How Prevalent Is Racism in Society?

Other titles in the *In Controversy* series:

Are Video Games Harmful?
Can Renewable Energy Replace Fossil Fuels?
Childhood Obesity
Does the Death Penalty Deter Crime?
Does Illegal Immigration Harm Society?
How Can Suicide Be Reduced?
How Dangerous Are Performance-Enhancing Drugs?
How Does Cell Phone Use Impact Teenagers?
How Serious a Problem Is Drug Use in Sports?
How Serious a Threat Is Climate Change?
How Should America Respond to Illegal Immigration?
How Should Sex Education Be Taught in Schools?
How Should the World Respond to Global Warming?
Identity Theft
Is Animal Experimentation Ethical?
Is the Death Penalty Just?
Is Human Embryo Experimentation Ethical?
Is Medical Marijuana Necessary?
Is Offshore Oil Drilling Worth the Risks?
Is Social Networking Beneficial to Society?
Is Stem Cell Research Necessary?
Is the World Prepared for a Deadly Influenza Pandemic?
Should the Drinking Age Be Lowered?
Should Juveniles Be Tried as Adults?
Should Marijuana Be Legalized?
Should Smoking Be Banned?
What Impact Does Mental Illness Have on Violent Crime?

How Prevalent Is Racism in Society?

Peggy J. Parks

IN CONTROVERSY

San Diego, CA

Special thanks to Marianne Case and Jennifer V. Tyler
for assistance with sidebar writing.

Printed in the United States

For more information, contact:
ReferencePoint Press, Inc.
PO Box 27779
San Diego, CA 92198
www. ReferencePointPress.com

LIBRARY OF CONGRESS CATALOGING-IN-PUBLICATION DATA

Parks, Peggy J., 1951-
How prevalent is racism in society? / by Peggy J. Parks.
pages cm. -- (In controversy series)
Includes bibliographical references and index.
Audience: Grade 9-12.
ISBN 978-1-60152-716-5 (hardback) -- ISBN 1-60152-716-0 (hardback)
1. Racism--United States--Juvenile literature. 2. United States--Race relations--Juvenile literature. 3. Discrimination in housing--United States--Juvenile literature. 4. Affirmative action programs--United States--Juvenile literature. I. Title.
E184.A1P326 2015
305.800973--dc23
2014015793

Contents

Foreword

In 2008, as the US economy and economies worldwide were falling into the worst recession since the Great Depression, most Americans had difficulty comprehending the complexity, magnitude, and scope of what was happening. As is often the case with a complex, controversial issue such as this historic global economic recession, looking at the problem as a whole can be overwhelming and often does not lead to understanding. One way to better comprehend such a large issue or event is to break it into smaller parts. The intricacies of global economic recession may be difficult to understand, but one can gain insight by instead beginning with an individual contributing factor, such as the real estate market. When examined through a narrower lens, complex issues become clearer and easier to evaluate.

This is the idea behind ReferencePoint Press's *In Controversy* series. The series examines the complex, controversial issues of the day by breaking them into smaller pieces. Rather than looking at the stem cell research debate as a whole, a title would examine an important aspect of the debate such as *Is Stem Cell Research Necessary?* or *Is Embryonic Stem Cell Research Ethical?* By studying the central issues of the debate individually, researchers gain a more solid and focused understanding of the topic as a whole.

Each book in the series provides a clear, insightful discussion of the issues, integrating facts and a variety of contrasting opinions for a solid, balanced perspective. Personal accounts and direct quotes from academic and professional experts, advocacy groups, politicians, and others enhance the narrative. Sidebars add depth to the discussion by expanding on important ideas and events. For quick reference, a list of key facts concludes every chapter. Source notes, an annotated organizations list, bibliography, and index provide student researchers with additional tools for papers and class discussion.

The *In Controversy* series also challenges students to think critically about issues, to improve their problem-solving skills, and to sharpen their ability to form educated opinions. As President Barack Obama stated in a March 2009 speech, success in the twenty-first century will not be measurable merely by students' ability to "fill in a bubble on a test but whether they possess 21st century skills like problem-solving and critical thinking and entrepreneurship and creativity." Those who possess these skills will have a strong foundation for whatever lies ahead.

No one can know for certain what sort of world awaits today's students. What we can assume, however, is that those who are inquisitive about a wide range of issues; open-minded to divergent views; aware of bias and opinion; and able to reason, reflect, and reconsider will be best prepared for the future. As the international development organization Oxfam notes, "Today's young people will grow up to be the citizens of the future: but what that future holds for them is uncertain. We can be quite confident, however, that they will be faced with decisions about a wide range of issues on which people have differing, contradictory views. If they are to develop as global citizens all young people should have the opportunity to engage with these controversial issues."

In Controversy helps today's students better prepare for tomorrow. An understanding of the complex issues that drive our world and the ability to think critically about them are essential components of contributing, competing, and succeeding in the twenty-first century.

Is Racism a Thing of the Past?

The date of August 28, 2013, was momentous in US history: it marked the fiftieth anniversary of one of the most famous speeches ever given. On that day in 1963, from the steps of the Lincoln Memorial in Washington, DC, the revered civil rights leader Martin Luther King Jr. delivered his "I Have a Dream" speech. It was an emotional, passionate plea for racism to end and for all people, regardless of their race, to be treated as equals. "I have a dream," King said, "that my four little children will one day live in a nation where they will not be judged by the color of their skin but by the content of their character."[1] Tragically, King was assassinated five years later, so he never knew if his dream of ending racism became reality—and that remains an unresolved issue today, even though decades have passed since his death.

Vastly Different Views

People often use the word *racism* interchangeably with terms such as *bigotry*, *discrimination*, and *prejudice*. Even though these terms are all related, racism has a much deeper meaning, one that is rooted in generations of oppression, superiority, and power. According to the Anti-Defamation League, racism is the belief that a particular race is superior or inferior to another, as the group explains: "It may be defined as the hatred of one person by another—or the belief that another person is less than human—because of skin color, language, customs, place of birth or any factor that supposedly reveals the basic nature of that person. It has influenced wars, slavery, the formation of nations, and legal codes."[2]

There are extremely diverse opinions about racism in the United States, with some people questioning whether it even still exists. Louisiana governor Bobby Jindal, for instance, is convinced that too much emphasis is placed on people's "separateness" rather than how race relations have improved over the years. He writes, "I do believe . . . that while racism still rears its ugly head from time to time, America has made significant progress in the half century since Dr. King's incredible speech." As an example of how far the country has progressed since the 1960s, Jindal cites the fact that he, the son of Indian immigrants, has won the gubernatorial election several times in a Deep South state that has long been known for its racist culture. "Here's what I've found in Louisiana," says Jindal. "The voters want to know what you believe, what you stand for, and what you plan to do, not what shade your skin is. And I think that's true of the country as a whole."[3]

"I have a dream that my four little children will one day live in a nation where they will not be judged by the color of their skin but by the content of their character."[1]

— Martin Luther King Jr., a renowned civil rights leader who was slain in 1968.

Jindal's opinion is not shared by everyone. Many believe racism is still a serious problem in the United States, and they contend that it must remain a major focus or it will never be resolved. Jessica Wong, an Asian American doctoral candidate at Duke University, has experienced what she calls "the oppressive weight of racial expectations and assumptions." She explains, "Some feel trivial, like the belief that because I'm Asian I must know kung fu, play a musical instrument or be good at math. Others feel heavier, like that of the exotic and sexually available Asian woman." According to Wong, such racial stereotypes are much more pervasive than people often realize—or are willing to admit. "They are wide reaching," she says, "showing up in the institutional structures of society—in the prison system, in our schools, in our job market. They become a part of the fabric of American social sensibility and, at times, find a way into our public policy. . . . Racism isn't a thing of the past."[4]

What the Public Thinks

According to an October 2012 Associated Press survey, the majority of Americans have beliefs that confirm Wong's claim about racism. Participants were asked to respond to a number of explicit questions about African Americans and Hispanics. More than half expressed negative attitudes about blacks and a slightly higher number felt negatively toward Hispanics. This finding was troubling for a number of reasons, says Alan Jenkins, director of the communications, research, and policy organization Opportunity Agenda: "That has very real circumstances in the way people are treated by police, the way kids are treated by teachers, the way home seekers are treated by landlords and real estate agents."[5]

A more recent survey that explored Americans' opinions about race-related issues was conducted by the Pew Research Center. More than twenty-two hundred white, black, and Hispanic adults were asked to share their opinions about progress toward racial equality in the United States. In the August 22, 2013, report of the survey, the authors conclude that overall, "racial equality remains an elusive goal." The report shows that only 45 percent of all Americans think significant progress has been made since the 1960s toward ending racism, as the authors explain: "The overwhelming majority says the slow and sometimes painful process of building a color-blind society remains largely unfinished business."[6]

A particularly interesting finding of the Pew survey was how varied opinions were among people of different races. When asked how much progress toward racial equality the United States has made in the past fifty years, nearly half of all whites said "a lot" of progress has been made compared with 43 percent of Hispanics and 32 percent of blacks. The disparity was even more pronounced when participants were asked how much more needs to be done to achieve King's dream of a society in which people of all races are considered equal. Nearly 80 percent of blacks said a lot more needs to be done, compared with 48 percent of Hispanics and 44 percent of whites.

Martin Luther King Jr. acknowledges the crowd on the occasion of his "I Have a Dream" speech in Washington, DC, in 1963. The speech was an impassioned plea for the end of racism and for equal treatment for all people regardless of race.

This disparity was also apparent when questions were asked about the treatment of black people in the participants' communities. Among white respondents, only 16 percent thought that black people were treated less fairly than whites in stores or restaurants, whereas 40 percent of Hispanics and more than half of black respondents felt this was the case. Similar differences of opinion were evident when questions were asked about treatment by police and the courts, in the workplace, when voting, when seeking health care, and at public schools—far more African Americans felt that people of their race were treated less fairly than whites.

"From the courtroom to the classroom to the voting booth," says the August 2013 report, "blacks are consistently more likely than whites to say blacks in their community are treated less fairly by key institutions."[7]

"We've Come a Long Way"

Since the 1960s, when Martin Luther King launched the American civil rights movement with his impassioned pleas for equality, the issue of racism has been embroiled in controversy. Today many people insist that it is no longer a pressing issue, whereas others could not disagree more. Hakeem Jeffries, a state assemblyman from New York, says that he is "cautiously optimistic" that the future will bring increased racial tolerance. "We've come a long way," he says, but based on findings from recent surveys, "clearly . . . there's a long way to go."[8]

Facts

- **According to an April 30, 2012, report by the National Fair Housing Alliance, people of color will constitute the majority of the US population within thirty years.**
- **In a November 2013 Episcopal Church survey, 69 percent of participants felt that African Americans were victims of discrimination, 63 percent felt that Hispanics were, and 51 percent felt that Native Americans were.**
- **A 2013 Pew Research poll gauging American attitudes toward Islam found that 42 percent of respondents think Islam is more likely than other religions to encourage the use of violence.**
- **According to the Southern Poverty Law Center, the number of active hate groups in the United States has more than doubled since 2002.**

CHAPTER ONE

What Are the Origins of the Racism Conflict?

From the time the first European settlers arrived on the shores of America, the millions of natives living there were assumed to be inferior to white people. This was evident in the derogatory way the natives were described: as savages, barbarians, or heathens. Convinced of their superiority, white settlers took it upon themselves to "civilize" the natives, whom they referred to as "Indians." The goal was to rid the natives of their culture and customs, and in the process make them look and behave more like white people. This perceived duty of whites to civilize Native Americans became known as "the white man's burden"—and was used as justification not only for changing the natives' ways but also for robbing them of their land. British explorer and naturalist John Lawson was one white man who found the treatment of native peoples deplorable, as he wrote in 1709:

> We look upon them with Scorn and Disdain, and think them little better than Beasts in Human Shape; though, if well examined, we shall find that for all our Religion and Education we possess more Moral Deformities and Evils than these Savages do, or are acquainted withal. We reckon them Slaves in Comparison to us, and Intruders, as oft as

> they enter our Houses, or hunt near our Dwellings. But if we will admit Reason to be our Guide, she will inform us that these *Indians* are the freest People in the World, and so far from being Intruders upon us, that we have abandon'd our own Native Soil to drive them out and possess theirs.[9]

The Trail of Tears

Lawson's sensitivity toward Native Americans was uncommon, and over time the Europeans' treatment of them grew more and more oppressive. As additional settlers arrived in America and claimed the new land as their home, the natives were increasingly viewed as an obstacle, inferior peoples who stood in the way of progress. Most whites were convinced that the land was rightfully theirs no matter who was living on it—so they took it. The social change group Do Something explains:

> In an effort to obtain much of North America as territory of the United States, a long series of wars, massacres, forced displacements . . . , restriction of food rights, and the imposition of treaties, land was taken and numerous hardships imposed. Ideologies justifying the context included stereotypes of Native Americans as 'merciless Indian savages' and the quasi-religious doctrine of manifest destiny which asserted divine blessing for U.S. conquest of all lands west of the Atlantic seaboard to the Pacific.[10]

By the early 1800s several Native American tribes were still living on millions of acres of land in the southeastern states of Georgia, Alabama, Tennessee, Mississippi, Kentucky, and North Carolina. As time went by, due to a series of laws passed by the US Congress and rulings by the Supreme Court, the natives lost all rights to land that had been theirs for generations. The final blow was a piece of legislation called the Indian Removal Act, which was signed into law by President Andrew Jackson in 1830. As the US Department of State Office of the Historian explains,

> The Act established a process whereby the President could grant land west of the Mississippi River to Indian tribes

The Jim Crow Era

The term *Jim Crow* refers to a series of laws, social norms, and rules of etiquette that governed the behavior of black Americans between the 1870s and mid-1960s. This racial caste system was most rigid in the South but was in place throughout the country. "Under Jim Crow," says Ferris State University sociology professor David Pilgrim, "African Americans were relegated to the status of second class citizens. Jim Crow represented the legitimization of anti-black racism." Most people are aware of highly publicized segregation tactics from that era, such as separate schools, separate seating areas on buses, and separate drinking fountains and restrooms. But there were numerous other rules that also governed black people's behavior. For instance, white motorists had the right-of-way at all intersections. Black people were not allowed to show affection toward one another in public. And a black man could not offer to shake hands with a white woman, since touching her could lead to accusations of rape.

Black Americans were expected to adhere to these and other societal norms without question—and those who dared to resist faced severe punishment. "Whites could physically beat blacks with impunity," says Pilgrim. "Blacks had little legal recourse against these assaults because the Jim Crow criminal justice system was all-white: police, prosecutors, judges, juries, and prison officials."

David Pilgrim, "What Was Jim Crow?," Ferris State University, 2012. www.ferris.edu.

that agreed to give up their homelands. As incentives, the law allowed the Indians financial and material assistance to travel to their new locations and start new lives and guaranteed that the Indians would live on their new property under the protection of the United States Government

Members of the Cherokee Nation, forced from their homes in the 1830s, make their way along the Trail of Tears. America's racist past began with its treatment of Native Americans.

forever. With the Act in place, Jackson and his followers were free to persuade, bribe, and threaten tribes into signing removal treaties and leaving the Southeast.[11]

Left with little choice but to comply with the mandate, tribal leaders from the Chickasaws, Choctaws, Creeks, Seminoles, and Cherokees signed treaties ceding their lands to the US government. On November 1, 1831, the Choctaws were the first tribe to begin the long, arduous journey west, which came to be known as the Trail of Tears.

A few tribes resisted the government takeover at first, such as the Cherokees, who occupied land in several southeastern states. They attempted to hold onto their land by working through legal channels, challenging in court the laws that restricted their freedom on lands that they rightfully owned. As hard as they fought, though, they had no chance of winning. In 1836 the Cherokees were given two years to vacate their land and migrate to regions west of the Mississippi River.

When the deadline arrived, only two thousand of the Cherokees had complied with the law, while the remaining sixteen thousand refused to leave. So the US government sent tens of thousands of military troops to forcibly remove them, dragging men, women, and children from their homes and throwing them into temporary holding pens known as stockades. One white man who witnessed this and was horrified by it was John Burnett, a soldier with the US Army. In the early 1800s Burnett had befriended many Cherokee people and lived among them for a while. Because he spoke their language, military officials used him as an interpreter as the Cherokees were taken off their land, and also when they were transported farther west. This journey began in October 1838, and Burnett called it "the blackest chapter on the pages of American history." He went on to describe what he had seen: "In the chill of a drizzling rain on an October morning I saw them loaded like cattle or sheep into six hundred and forty-five wagons and started toward the west. . . . When the bugle sounded and the wagons started rolling many of the children rose to their feet and waved their little hands good-by to their mountain homes, knowing they were leaving them forever."[12]

> "The trail of the exiles was a trail of death. . . . And covetousness on the part of the white race was the cause of all that the Cherokees had to suffer."[13]
>
> —John Burnett, a soldier with the US Army who befriended the Cherokees in the early 1800s.

The grueling cross-country journey lasted more than five months, finally coming to an end in late March 1839. Over that time the natives endured brutal, inhumane conditions, and as many as four thousand died along the way. Referring to "4000 silent graves," Burnett wrote, "The trail of the exiles was a trail of death. . . . And covetousness on the part of the white race was the cause of all that the Cherokees had to suffer."[13]

The Scourge of Human Enslavement

As America's growing population continued to spread into land that formerly belonged to the natives, their world changed so drastically that they barely recognized it. This was also a period when other races were being exploited for the benefit of white settlers, as a PBS documentary explains:

> European explorers not only ventured to the lands and natural wealth of the Americas. They also traveled to Africa, where

they began a trans-Atlantic slave trade that would bring millions of Africans to the Americas as well. This slave trade would over time lead to a new social and economic system: one where the color of one's skin could determine whether he or she might live as a free citizen or be enslaved for life.[14]

One Courageous American

In 1942, based on an executive order signed by the president, all immigrants of Japanese ancestry were ordered to live in internment camps. Tens of thousands of people were forced to leave their homes and move to the prison-like camps. One of the few people who dared to resist was Fred Korematsu, a twenty-three-year-old Japanese American who had been born in Oakland, California. On May 30, 1942, Korematsu was arrested and convicted of defying the order to report for internment. He appealed the constitutionality of his conviction on the grounds that it was motivated by racism. His appeal went all the way to the US Supreme Court, but the justices ruled against him. They refuted his claim of racism and stated that the internments were necessary to protect the country during wartime.

For years Korematsu maintained his innocence. Finally, in 1983, a presidential commission concluded that the internments of Japanese Americans were indeed fueled by racial prejudice. Researchers also found intelligence agency memos that had been suppressed during the Supreme Court case. The memos made it clear that Japanese Americans had been unjustly forced into the camps. Korematsu's conviction was overturned, and he became a renowned civil rights activist. In 1998 President Bill Clinton awarded him the Presidential Medal of Freedom. Korematsu died in 2005, and five years later the state of California honored him by declaring January 30, his birthday, to be Fred Korematsu Day.

Although the practice of slavery had existed for thousands of years, slaves were first brought to the colonies in 1619. In the English colony of Jamestown, Virginia, settlers were desperate to grow enough food and also saw great potential for growing tobacco and cotton. Doing that would require many laborers to work in the fields, and the settlers thought that using slaves would be the perfect solution.

In 1619 the first slave ship arrived in Jamestown carrying twenty African passengers who had been kidnapped from their native villages. The late historian Howard Zinn wrote,

> The marches to the [African] coast, sometimes for 1,000 miles, with people shackled around the neck, under whip and gun, were death marches, in which two of every five blacks died. On the coast, they were kept in cages until they were picked and sold. . . . Then they were packed aboard the slave ships, in spaces not much bigger than coffins, chained together in the dark, wet slime of the ship's bottom, choking in the stench of their own excrement.[15]

Conditions onboard the ships were so appalling that about one-third of the slaves died before reaching America. Still, slave traders reaped huge profits from selling the survivors, so the slave trade began to flourish.

Over the next 150 years, use of slave labor became a common practice in America. In his book *Inhuman Bondage: The Rise and Fall of Slavery in the New World*, historian David Brion Davis writes that on the "eve of the American Revolution" in 1770, slavery was legal and rarely challenged. "The ghastly slave trade from Africa was still expanding," says Davis, "and for many decades had been shipping five Africans across the Atlantic for every European immigrant to the Americas. An imaginary 'hemispheric traveler' would have seen black slaves in every colony from Canada and New England all the way south to Spanish Peru and Chile."[16]

As widespread as the practice of slavery was, it was most prevalent in the South, where cotton and tobacco were the primary crops. A History.com documentary

"The marches to the coast, sometimes for 1,000 miles, with people shackled around the neck, under whip and gun, were death marches, in which two of every five blacks died."[15]

—The late historian Howard Zinn, referring to Africans being kidnapped to be sold as slaves.

titled *Slavery in America,* explains: "Slavery itself was never widespread in the North, though many of the region's businessmen grew rich on the slave trade and investments in southern plantations. Between 1774 and 1804, all of the northern states abolished slavery, but the so-called 'peculiar institution' remained absolutely vital to the South."[17] By 1860 the slave population in the United States reached nearly 4 million, with more than half of these individuals living in the Southern states. Then in November of that year, Abraham Lincoln was elected as president of the United States. Because he was opposed to slavery, Southerners viewed him as a threat to their way of life. Over the following months and into the next year, eleven Southern states seceded from the Union to form the Confederate States of America.

This secession caused enormous conflict among the states and ultimately led to the Civil War, which lasted from 1861 to 1865. By the time the war was over, more than six hundred thousand soldiers were dead, and thousands more were left injured. But as bloody as the war had been, African Americans were finally free, and this was finalized with passage of the Thirteenth Amendment in 1865. The Fourteenth Amendment, which granted former slaves the rights of citizenship, followed in 1868, and two years later the Fifteenth Amendment gave them the right to vote. But African Americans still faced a multitude of challenges, as History.com explains: "The provisions of the Constitution were often ignored or violated, and it was difficult for former slaves to gain a foothold in the post-war economy thanks to restrictive black codes and regressive contractual arrangements such as sharecropping."[18]

Stripped of Freedom

In the decades following the Civil War, people from all over the world continued to flock to the United States. Many immigrants came from Japan, leaving an unstable country in hopes of finding peace and prosperity elsewhere. By the dawn of the twentieth century an estimated 120,000 Japanese had settled in the United States, mostly in cities and towns along the Pacific coast. But in 1941, their lives were shattered in what a Library of Congress historical document calls "one of the 20th century's worst crimes against civil liberties."[19] This happened because they were blamed for hostile actions by Japan over which they had no control.

On the morning of December 7, 1941, Japan launched a devastating surprise attack on the United States. Several hundred Japanese warplanes struck the US naval base at Pearl Harbor, Hawaii, causing massive destruction and killing more than twenty-four hundred Americans. As news of the attack spread to America's West Coast, police began to surround neighborhoods where Japanese Americans were living. Those of Japanese heritage were considered adversaries of the United States, even if they were American citizens. Thousands of people were arrested in a very short time. Then, seventy-four days after the Pearl Harbor attack, President Franklin D. Roosevelt signed Executive Order 9066, which mandated the forced imprisonment of Japanese Americans. In his book *Japanese Americans: The Formation and Transformations of an Ethnic Group*, author and historian Paul Spickard writes, "Husbands and fathers

A family of Japanese Americans from California awaits a bus that will take them to an internment camp in 1942. Thousands of Japanese Americans were interned during World War II because they were perceived to be a security threat.

were taken from their families suddenly, without explanation and without charge. Most did not see their families again until months later, when they were reunited behind barbed wire."[20]

Initially the US Department of War ordered all Japanese who were living on the West Coast to relocate immediately, but most could not make such a move on short notice. Those who were able to travel east quickly found that they were not wanted, and they faced widespread racism. Chase Clark, the governor of Idaho, did not hesitate to express his bigotry toward Japanese people who might consider moving to the state: "The Japs live like rats, breed like rats and act like rats," Chase said. "We don't want them buying or leasing land or becoming permanently located in our state."[21]

"The Japs live like rats, breed like rats and act like rats. We don't want them buying or leasing land or becoming permanently located in our state."[21]

— Chase Clark, who was governor of Idaho during the forced relocation of Japanese Americans in the early 1940s.

Ultimately, efforts to pressure Japanese citizens to move voluntarily were largely unsuccessful. So, in an eerie reminder of the Trail of Tears a century before, more than one hundred thousand Japanese immigrants, half of whom were children, were forcibly moved to desolate areas in states such as Wyoming, Idaho, Utah, Colorado, and Arizona. Once there, they were ordered to live in internment camps, which were prison-like areas surrounded by barbed wire and guarded by soldiers armed with machine guns. One Japanese American who experienced this was George Takei, an actor best known for his role as Sulu on the original *Star Trek* television series. He and his family were forced into an internment camp in southeast Arkansas. "We happened to look like the people that bombed Pearl Harbor," says Takei, "and put in prison camps simply because of our race."[22]

Although Takei was only five years old at the time, the experience is still vivid in his mind. "I went to school and began every school-day morning with the pledge of allegiance [to] the flag," he says. "I could see the barbed wire fence and the sentry tower right outside my schoolhouse window as I recited the words, 'With liberty and justice for all.' The stinging irony meant nothing to me—I was a child."[23] Takei and his family lived in the camp for three years. When they moved back to Los Angeles, they had an extremely difficult time. Even though they were no longer prisoners, they suffered the widespread discrimination against Japanese Americans that was still rampant.

Unfair and Discriminatory

Their experience echoed that of people who had emigrated from China during the mid-nineteenth century. When word spread that gold had been discovered in California in 1848, thousands of Chinese made the treacherous sixty-day journey across the Pacific Ocean in search of better lives. Once they arrived in the United States, they quickly became known for their willingness to work hard. Author Henry Kittredge Norton wrote about this in a book published in 1924:

> The Chinese were surely in a land of milk and honey. They had left a land of war and starvation where work could not be had and food must be begged and here they found themselves in the midst of work and plenty. They were everywhere welcomed and their wages were such that they could save a substantial part to send back to the families they had left at home in China; or, if they did not wish to labor for masters, they could go to the mines. Here they could take an old claim which had been abandoned by the white miner and dig from it gold dust which to them represented wealth untold.[24]

By the 1870s an estimated 150,000 Chinese were living in the United States, and white Americans were growing increasingly resentful of them. An economic downturn had resulted in serious unemployment, and frustrated workers blamed Chinese immigrants (whom they already considered inferior) for taking jobs that should "rightfully" go to white people. This led to massive protests, many of which turned violent, and ultimately resulted in legislation designed to curtail Chinese people from entering the country. Known as the Chinese Exclusion Act of 1882, the law halted Chinese immigration for ten years. In addition, it prohibited Chinese who were already liv-

"The Chinese were surely in a land of milk and honey."[24]

— Henry Kittredge Norton, an author who wrote about discrimination against Chinese immigrants during the 1800s.

ing in the United States from becoming citizens. Laws passed in subsequent years extended the ban on Chinese immigration even further, and it was not until the 1940s that people from China were once again allowed to make their homes in "the land of milk and honey."

A Tumultuous History

The United States is often called a melting pot because of the wide variety of people who have settled there and made it their home. But during many periods throughout history, not everyone in America was treated fairly; in fact, some endured blatant racism and severe cruelty simply because of the color of their skin. This was true of Native Americans, whose land was taken from them by white settlers, and Africans who were kidnapped from their homes and forced into slavery. Japanese and Chinese immigrants also encountered racist treatment by whites who believed them to be inferior. Today many people are shocked to discover how much of a role racism has played in America's history. As shocking as that history is, though, it could be a positive thing, as remembering the sordid events from the past might prevent them from ever being repeated in the future.

Facts

- **According to the late historian George M. Fredrickson, the identification of the Jews with the devil and witchcraft during the thirteenth and fourteenth centuries was likely the first sign of a racist view of the world.**
- **During the early twentieth century the Racial Integrity Act made it a crime in the United States for whites to marry anyone with even a trace of African American ancestry.**

- Ferris State University sociology professor David Pilgrim states that during the Jim Crow era (1877 to the mid-1960s) a law passed in Birmingham, Alabama, made it illegal for black and white people to play checkers or dominoes together.
- During the 1800s physician and anthropologist Samuel George Morton unsuccessfully tried to prove that select races were superior to others by measuring the brain size of white people, black people, and Native Americans.
- According to the late author Thomas S. Gossett, during the early twentieth century some churches in the United States hung a pine slab on the door; only those whose skin was lighter than the color of the wood were allowed to enter.
- The social change group Do Something says that during the 1800s and early 1900s Jews and Italians who immigrated to the United States were viewed as nonwhite and were subject to extreme prejudice and racism.

CHAPTER TWO

How Common Is Racial Profiling in Law Enforcement?

A Washington, DC, organization called Rights Working Group (RWG) exists to protect the civil liberties and human rights of Americans. In a March 2013 article, RWG communications manager Keith Rushing discusses racial profiling, which involves being mistrustful and suspicious of people based on their race, ethnicity, religion, or national origin. "At its core," says Rushing, "racial profiling is about racism and stereotypes and assuming the worst of people based on a biased perception of reality that is then projected and multiplied, affecting and endangering everyone of that same race, ethnicity, nationality or religion." He goes on to explain that in terms of law enforcement, officers use these same factors when making decisions about "whom to investigate, arrest or detain absent evidence of a specific crime or criminal behavior."[25]

Stop-and-Frisk

Rushing makes it clear that even though African Americans have a long history of being racially profiled, they are by no means the only ones. People of many different races, religions, and ethnicities have experienced it and continue to do so. In many cases no one ever knows about it—and even when it is known, action is rarely taken. According to Rushing, a major priority for the RWG is to "keep the spotlight on racial profiling"[26] with the goal of banning it. There are, however, innumerable challenges involved with such a goal. Because of the discord over when racial profiling is, and is not, present, attempting to ban it would be a formidable task.

> "Racial profiling is about racism and stereotypes and assuming the worst of people based on a biased perception of reality."[25]
>
> — Keith Rushing, communications manager with the civil liberties organization Rights Working Group.

An example of this is the controversy over a law enforcement policy called stop, question, and frisk, or as it is commonly known, stop-and-frisk. Under this program, which was first implemented in New York City in September 1971, police officers who have reason to suspect that someone is involved in (or has been involved in) a serious crime have the authority to stop him or her and ask questions. If the situation seems to warrant it, police may frisk the person. In a March 2014 *Atlantic* article, journalist Daniel Bergner describes the purpose of stop-and-frisk programs:

> They aim to get guns off the street, to glean information and solve crime sprees, and, perhaps above all, to act as a deterrent, by letting criminals and would-be lawbreakers know that they might find themselves getting a pat-down at any given moment. Arguably, the policies have succeeded, helping to cut crime dramatically from New York to Los Angeles. But they have also stirred the loudest and most painful present debate in American criminology: Are young men of color being unfairly—and unconstitutionally—singled out?[27]

If, in fact, it is proved that police have singled out individuals solely because of race, this could be a violation of the US Constitution's Fourth Amendment. It guarantees citizens the right to be free from searches or other personal invasions without probable cause.

Controversy in New York

Although stop-and-frisk programs are used throughout the United States, New York City's has received the most publicity. One New

Police question a group of young black men in the Brownsville neighborhood of Brooklyn, New York, where stop-and-frisk is a common occurrence. Some New Yorkers applaud the program for reducing crime while others criticize it for encouraging police to harass people of color.

Yorker who fully supports the tactic is Deborah Richardson, a black postal worker in her sixties. For more than fourteen years Richardson delivered mail in east Brooklyn's Brownsville area, which has the highest concentration of public housing in the United States. "I'd like to see more stops and frisks," she says. "This is a dangerous neighborhood." Pointing at one of the towering housing complexes where she once pushed a mail cart, she adds, "I won't even go up in those monstrosities anymore."[28]

Another avid supporter of stop-and-frisk is former New York City mayor Michael Bloomberg, who credits the program for the city's significant drop in violent crime. Bloomberg is adamant that stop-and-frisk is not an example of racial profiling, which he wholeheartedly agrees is wrong. "Here are the facts," he says. "In 2004, I signed a law banning racial profiling. Police Commissioner Ray Kelly and I have zero tolerance for it. We have worked hard to strengthen police-community relations, which are better today than at any point since the 1960s. Part of that work has involved giving black and Latino community leaders what they demand and deserve: a stronger police presence."[29]

Opponents of stop-and-frisk see things differently. Rather than merely a stronger police presence in high-crime areas, they view stop-and-frisk as a way of giving officers free rein to detain minorities without having reasonable suspicion of criminal activity or wrongdoing—meaning no probable cause. One young black man who has experienced this over and over again is Jamal Richards, who is from New York's Brooklyn borough. Now a student at Buffalo State College, when Richards was a teenager and living at home he was stopped by police four or five times a week. He is convinced that he was singled out solely because of his race since never once when he was stopped was he doing anything wrong. It made life difficult and stressful much of the time, causing him to fear that he was always being watched, even in his own neighborhood. "You constantly have this negative eye on you just waiting for you to mess up," he says. "As if you're already in the pipeline to prison."[30]

"In 2004, I signed a law banning racial profiling. Police Commissioner Ray Kelly and I have zero tolerance for it."[29]

— Former New York City mayor Michael Bloomberg.

Richards is far from being the only one who feels this way. Thousands of New Yorkers, mostly young black or Hispanic men, have also complained about being harassed by police on a regular basis. They too are convinced that the only reason they were singled out was because of their race or ethnicity. Research—including data from the New York Police Department (NYPD)—suggests that this accusation might be valid. According to the American Civil Liberties Union (ACLU), NYPD reports show that between 2002 and 2012 more than 5 million people were stopped in the city, with 4.3 million of them either black or Hispanic. In nearly 90 percent of the cases, police found that the suspects were innocent of any wrongdoing. Records also show that New Yorkers were stopped by the police nearly two hundred thousand times in 2013. Of those who were detained, 56 percent were black, 29 percent were Hispanic, and 11 percent were white; again, nearly 90 percent were found to be innocent of any crime.

Bloomberg says there is a valid reason why police officers stop and question minorities more than whites, as he explains: "The

A Counterproductive Tactic?

Opponents of New York City's stop-and-frisk program warn that it causes young men and women of color to distrust police. This was the finding of a study released in September 2013 by the Vera Institute of Justice. The researchers interviewed young people in six highly patrolled, high-crime areas who had been stopped at least once. Two groups of primarily black and Hispanic youth were surveyed: 474 between the ages of eighteen and twenty-five, and 42 aged thirteen to twenty-one.

The study found that 44 percent of the participants had been stopped nine times or more, but less than one-third were told why they were stopped. Nearly half reported being threatened by police and/or experiencing physical force at the hands of an officer. One of the most troubling findings was that trust in police and willingness to cooperate with them is extremely low. Nearly 90 percent of youth believe that residents of their neighborhood do not trust the police and only one in four would report someone who they believe had committed a crime. The study authors write,

> The experience of being stopped repeatedly, coupled with the perception among the young people surveyed that they are unfairly targeted, turns out to have serious consequences for public safety. . . . The more often young people are stopped, the less likely they are to trust and cooperate with law enforcement by reporting crimes. So when police stop an individual numerous times, those actions have a clear cost.

Jennifer Fratello, Andrés F. Rengifo, and Jennifer Trone, "Coming of Age with Stop and Frisk: Experiences, Self-Perceptions, and Public Safety Implications," Vera Institute of Justice, September 2013. www.vera.org.

NYPD targets its manpower to the areas that suffer the highest crime levels. Ninety percent of all people killed in our city—and 90 percent of all those who commit the murders and other violent crimes—are black and Hispanic."[31] NYPD crime data verify Bloomberg's assertion that minorities are disproportionately involved in the city's violent crime. But opponents of stop-and-frisk continue to argue that it is the wrong solution because it represents racial profiling.

Floyd v. City of New York

A federal judge shares that perspective, according to a ruling announced in August 2013. US district judge Shira A. Scheindlin ruled that the NYPD was using a policy of "indirect" racial profiling, which led to officers routinely stopping African Americans and Hispanics "who would not have been stopped if they were white." She went on to say that innocent people were being demeaned and humiliated: "No one should live in fear of being stopped whenever he leaves his home to go about the activities of daily life. Those who are routinely subjected to stops are overwhelmingly people of color, and they are justifiably troubled to be singled out when many of them have done nothing to attract the unwanted attention."[32]

Scheindlin's statements were in response to a federal class-action lawsuit filed on behalf of lead plaintiff David Floyd. An African American man from New York's Bronx borough, Floyd was first stopped by three police officers in April 2007. They demanded his identification, and when he handed it to them, they started patting him down from his groin to his ankle on both legs. Floyd informed the officers that he had not consented to the search, but they did not stop patting him down. Floyd was distraught over being treated like a criminal and says he felt "frustrated, humiliated—because it was on my block where I live, and I wasn't doing anything."[33]

Less than a year later, Floyd was subjected to another stop-and-frisk by NYPD officers. This time he was standing at the door of his apartment building holding a ring of keys and trying to help a neighbor who had locked himself out. "Before we could go in, we were stopped," says Floyd. Again the officers asked for identification, and again they patted him down from his groin to his ankles—once more without his permission. "It was again the humiliation," says Floyd, who began to feel hesitant about even going outside. "I felt that I was being told I shouldn't leave my home."[34]

In 2008 the Center for Constitutional Rights filed a lawsuit against the NYPD and the City of New York on behalf of Floyd. Several months later the suit was amended to a class-action suit, representing thousands of black and Hispanic New Yorkers who said they had been unlawfully stopped by police solely because of their race. The complicated lawsuit dragged on for more than five years, finally coming to a close on August 12, 2013. When Scheindlin announced her ruling, she did not order an end to the stop-and-frisk program. Rather, she ruled that some major changes needed to be implemented. In her statement, Scheindlin writes,

> I will order remedies, including immediate changes to the NYPD's policies, a joint-remedial process to consider further reforms, and the appointment of an independent monitor to oversee compliance with the remedies ordered in this case. I conclude with a particularly apt quote: "The idea of universal suspicion without individual evidence is what Americans find abhorrent and what black men in America must constantly fight. It is pervasive in policing policies—like stop-and-frisk, and . . . neighborhood watch—regardless of the collateral damage done to the majority of innocents. It's like burning down a house to rid it of mice."[35]

Driving While Black

Whether it applies to stop-and-frisk programs or not, racial profiling has been cited as a problem in cities and towns throughout the United States. Black people who believe they have been subjected to it during traffic stops have a derisive term for their alleged offense: *driving while black*. This is a wordplay on alcohol-related offenses such as driving while intoxicated and driving under the influence. Cornell University's Charlie Brown and Amanda Jantzi write,

David Floyd sued the City of New York and the New York Police Department over their stop-and-frisk policy. The federal judge who heard the case ruled that the policy was a form of racial profiling that demeaned and humiliated innocent people.

> The invention of the fictitious offense 'Driving While Black' captures the popular perception that police officers target African-Americans for traffic stops and are more likely to search an African-American's vehicle. This perception, however, is more than mere speculation; empirical research has tended to show that African-American drivers are more likely to be stopped and searched than drivers of other races.[36]

A yearlong study released in September 2013 shows that police officers in Kalamazoo, Michigan, were stopping black motorists far more often than white motorists. The study, which was conducted by a professional consulting firm, involved reviewing traffic stop data from March 1, 2012, to February 28, 2013. Eleven areas throughout the city were chosen for evaluation based on several factors, including the high number of stops at each. The study found that depending on the location, black drivers were stopped from 1.5 times to 3 times as often as whites. Another finding was that relative to the high number of black drivers who were stopped, they received fewer police citations than did white drivers. Blacks, however, were far more likely to be asked to exit their vehicles, to be searched, and to be handcuffed. The study also revealed that even though black motorists were searched far more often than whites, whites were more likely to be carrying contraband in their vehicles.

In response to the study, Kalamazoo chief of police Jeff Hadley stated that the findings and recommendations would be used to create an action plan. Six months later he announced that the plan was complete and in place, and he believed that his department had made progress toward eliminating racial profiling. The number of traffic stops had been cut nearly in half. Officers began concentrating on directed patrols, under which they focus on neighborhoods or sections of the city that are known for high levels of crime. In addition, the department launched a new consent-to-search policy, which Hadley says is meant to avoid what he calls "fishing expeditions." He explains, "Sometimes you have young, aggressive officers trying to do good work but can go too far. We have to guide and help them."[37] Hadley emphasizes that his department will continue to work toward eliminating racial profiling in hopes of regaining the trust of people in the community.

A Profiling Nightmare

Even as racial profiling continues to be challenged, various forms of it are still in practice throughout the United States. For instance, in the years since the September 11, 2001, terrorist attacks, profiling of Americans based on ethnicity and religion has increased. Rushing writes, "After 9/11, people who are Arab, Muslim and South Asian have found themselves routinely being singled out for secondary searches and interrogations when crossing international borders and entering and exiting the country."[38] Shoshana Hebshi, a journalist of mixed Arab-Jewish heritage, knows what it is like to be profiled because of her ethnicity, and what she went through was terrifying.

On September 11, 2011, the tenth anniversary of the terrorist attacks on the United States, Hebshi boarded a plane in Denver, Colorado, that was headed to Detroit, Michigan. "Silly me," she says. "I thought flying on 9/11 would be easy. I figured most people would choose not to fly that day so lines would be short, planes would be lightly filled and though security might be ratcheted up, we'd all feel safer knowing we had come a long way since that dreadful Tuesday morning 10 years ago."[39] Hebshi was seated next to two Indian American men whom she did not know. Sometime after the plane was airborne each of the men went to the restroom, which caused some passengers to become suspicious. They complained to the flight attendants, who in turn alerted the captain.

"Sometimes you have young, aggressive officers trying to do good work but can go too far. We have to guide and help them."[37]

— Jeff Hadley, chief of police in Kalamazoo, Michigan.

When the plane landed in Detroit, it remained on the tarmac as though the captain were waiting to have his gate cleared. Then, in a stern voice, he warned all passengers to stay in their seats while he moved the plane to a remote section of the airport, which was when Hebshi knew that something was very wrong. Police cars and vans with flashing lights followed the plane as it taxied and surrounded it when it came to a stop. Suddenly a team of FBI agents wielding machine guns stormed the plane and ran down the aisle, yelling for everyone to put their hands on the seat in front of them. The agents ordered Hebshi and the two men to get up and clamped handcuffs on their wrists. The three were then escorted off the plane, taken down the stairs, and pushed into waiting vehicles. "They wouldn't even tell me what was going on," says Hebshi, choking back tears. "No one would answer me." They arrived at an offsite building and were taken to separate cells. Under close observation by a female officer, Hebshi was told to strip naked, squat, and cough. "I was frightened and humiliated,"[40] she says. Hebshi was held and interrogated for more than four hours before finally being released. An officer took her back to her car, and she left to drive home to her family.

In 2013 Hebshi and the ACLU filed a lawsuit against a number of defendants, including the FBI, Frontier Airlines, Detroit Metro Airport Police, and the Transportation Security Administration. The suit alleges that Hebshi's constitutional protections against unreasonable search and seizure and discrimination were violated.

Harassed in Miami

Miami Gardens is a city in southeastern Florida located midway between Miami and Fort Lauderdale. Its population is predominantly lower middle class and about 95 percent African American and Hispanic. Like many cities of its size, Miami Gardens sees more than its fair share of crime. But at a little family market known as the 207 Quickstop, most of the problems are caused by police. The store's owner, Alex Saleh, is fed up. One of his employees, Earl Sampson, is a twenty-eight-year-old black man who has worked at the store for four years. Over that time he has been stopped and questioned 258 times. Of those stops, he was searched more than 100 times and jailed 56 times. Sampson was also arrested 62 times for trespassing—as though he could "trespass" at his own place of employment.

Although Sampson is the most extreme example of police harassment at the 207 Quickstop, many others have also been victims. The market is located in a poor minority neighborhood, and Saleh is proud of the friendly, trusting relationships he has built with his customers. After witnessing daily harassment of people who work and/or shop at his store, he became outraged and installed a surveillance system to keep tabs on the police. In 2013, armed with dozens of videos, Saleh sued the Miami Gardens Police Department for civil rights violations.

Her attorney, Bill Goodman, says that what happened to her was senseless and inexcusable. "She went through the whole operation of being screened, went in metal detectors and all the rest of it when she got on the plane," says Goodman. "And now she's forced to do this humiliating, embarrassing kind of horrible thing for having done absolutely nothing outside of the fact that her father was from Saudi Arabia. That was it."[41]

> *"Imagine a world where officers don't see a criminal whenever a child is leaving school or playing in the park."*[42]
>
> — Jamal Richards, a black college student from New York City who has been stopped by police multiple times for no apparent reason.

Daring to Hope

Evidence strongly suggests that racial profiling is an unfortunate fact of life for minorities throughout the United States. These people represent a highly diverse population, but the one thing they all share in common is that they look different from Caucasians. There is positive news, though: Public awareness of racial profiling is growing, and programs are being implemented by law enforcement to remedy the problem. Jamal Richards is an optimistic young man who is not afraid to dream about a time when racial profiling no longer exists. "Imagine a world where officers don't see a criminal whenever a child is leaving school or playing in the park," he says. "Where they see something positive instead of something negative."[42] Richards and other like-minded individuals hope that dream becomes reality in the not-too-distant future.

Facts

- According to the Center for Constitutional Rights, Hispanics and African Americans make up 23 and 29 percent (respectively) of New York City's population, yet they account for 84 percent of the individuals stopped under the city's stop-and-frisk program.

- A study by the New York Civil Liberties Union found that the NYPD stopped and frisked approximately 533,000 men in 2012, and 87 percent were black or Hispanic.

- According to legislative attorney Jody Feder, if race or ethnicity is one factor in a police officer's decision to stop someone, but not the only reason, this may not be a Fourteenth Amendment violation.

- An ACLU report released in June 2013 found that marijuana usage rates are roughly the same for black and white Americans, but blacks are nearly four times more likely to be arrested for possession than whites.

- In January 2014 US attorney general Eric Holder announced that the Justice Department would revise its stance on racial profiling to restrict officers from considering religion, national origin, gender, and sexual orientation in their investigations.

How Serious a Problem Is Housing Discrimination?

In the United States it is illegal for home sellers, landlords, banks, realtors, or anyone else associated with housing to discriminate against buyers or renters. That does not mean that all Americans feel free to live wherever they choose. Despite the fact that housing discrimination has been prohibited for nearly fifty years, studies by the US Department of Housing and Urban Development (HUD) and other agencies show that minorities still encounter it often. Because of that, it is much more difficult for them to find nice places to live than it is for whites. "For individuals and families," says Fred Freiberg, cofounder and executive director of the Fair Housing Justice Center, "it limits their housing choices, it dictates where you can and cannot live, and that means limited access to other opportunities: educational opportunities, employment opportunities, health care services, other amenities. It sustains and enforces patterns of racial segregation and poverty concentration, and it creates a whole host of inequalities that we could, frankly, do without."[43]

When Discrimination Was Legal

Although it is of little consolation to people who encounter housing discrimination today, the situation years ago was far, far worse for minorities. In the early twentieth century, for instance, not only was racial segregation legal, it was actually encouraged by the government with its enforcement of formal agreements known as covenants. These racially restrictive covenants, which were typically included in property deeds, controlled how property could be developed or used—as well as who would be allowed to live on the property. The Leadership Conference on Civil and Human Rights explains,

"By the 1920s, deeds in nearly every new housing development in the North prevented the use or ownership of homes by anyone other than 'the Caucasian race.'"[44]

—The Leadership Conference on Civil and Human Rights, which exists to protect the rights of all persons in the United States.

> By the 1920s, deeds in nearly every new housing development in the North prevented the use or ownership of homes by anyone other than "the Caucasian race." Many new homes still recorded racially restrictive covenants even after the Supreme Court held them unenforceable in 1948. As a result, people of color were excluded from many communities, limiting where they could settle and beginning the trend toward increased segregation. During the 1920s, property values became tied to race as a means to legitimize racial exclusion and protect racial boundaries.[44]

By the 1930s most American cities had designated boundaries within which people of color were allowed to live. Real estate agents fully supported this, as one wrote: "It's a sort of unwritten code that respectable real estate brokers should guide people into the areas where they'll fit in socially and keep them out of areas where they won't. Everybody's happier that way."[45] Although a number of federal agencies were established to help increase home ownership among Americans, this did not level the playing field for minorities. According to the Leadership Conference, only whites benefited from the housing programs created by these agencies:

> For example, to "assist" with lending decisions, the Federal Housing Authority prepared "neighborhood security

maps" that were based largely on the racial, ethnic, and economic status of residents. Indeed, a national trade association explicitly stated that minorities caused adverse influences upon a neighborhood. The American Institute of Real Estate Appraisers began using a ranking system that assessed risk based on the racial composition of the community, with English, Germans, Scotch, Irish, Scandinavians ranked at the top of the list and "Negroes" and "Mexicans" ranked at the bottom of the list. Lending institutions and the federal government employed underwriting guidelines that favored racially White, homogenous neighborhoods and led to the creation of a separate and unequal lending and financial system.[46]

One shady moneymaking tactic commonly used by real estate agents in the early twentieth century was known as blockbusting or panic peddling. This practice was intended to trigger the turnover of property and homes owned by whites to African Americans who were eager to buy a home. At the root of this practice was provoking white homeowners to fear that their property values were about to plummet. They were cautioned about the nearby location of black communities and were urged to sell quickly before it was too late. New Orleans historian and author Arnold R. Hirsch writes, "Agents frequently hired African American subagents and other individuals to walk or drive through changing areas soliciting business and otherwise behaving in such a manner as to provoke and exaggerate white fears."[47]

"Agents frequently hired African American subagents and other individuals to walk or drive through changing areas soliciting business and otherwise behaving in such a manner as to provoke and exaggerate white fears."[47]

— New Orleans historian and author Arnold R. Hirsch.

Panic peddlers often succeeded at scaring whites into selling their homes. Once that happened, they turned around and sold the homes for overinflated prices to African Americans who, as Hirsch writes, "faced painfully limited choices and inflated prices in a discriminatory housing market. Often providing financing and stringent terms to a captive audience, the blockbuster could realize substantial profits." The practice of blockbusting had several effects. A seemingly positive effect was that it enabled black people

Signs like these appeared in neighborhoods in Hollywood, California, in the 1920s. During this era, racial segregation was legal and even enforced by the government.

to own homes at a time when mainstream real estate and financial institutions refused to accommodate them. But blockbusting also led to widespread segregation, which Hirsch says "destabilized residential communities as it maximized racial tensions and fears."[48]

The Fair Housing Act

Although the Supreme Court made several rulings that banned the exclusion of minorities from certain geographic areas of cities, this did not end housing discrimination. In the late 1960s racial segregation was still rampant throughout the United States. Organizations such as the National Association for the Advancement of Colored People (NAACP) and the National Committee Against Discrimination in Housing began to lobby for the government to pass fair housing legislation.

The end result came to be known as the Fair Housing Act of

1968, which expanded on the historic Civil Rights Act of 1964. A History.com documentary explains:

> The bill's original goal was to extend federal protection to civil rights workers, but it was eventually expanded to address racial discrimination in housing. Title VIII of the proposed Civil Rights Act was known as the Fair Housing Act, later used as a shorthand description for the entire bill. It prohibited discrimination concerning the sale, rental and financing of housing based on race, religion, national origin and sex.[49]

After a fierce debate in both houses of Congress, the Fair Housing Act was signed into law on April 11, 1968. President Lyndon B. Johnson stated that its passage was a fitting tribute to Martin Luther King Jr., who had worked hard for fair housing for minorities and had been assassinated one week before the law was signed.

The Fair Housing Act was a major milestone in progress toward resolving housing discrimination, but it was only the first step in a long, complicated process. Over the following years housing remained segregated in many areas of the United States. "From 1950 to 1980," says History.com, "the total black population in America's urban centers increased from 6.1 million to 15.3 million. During this same time period, white Americans steadily moved out of the cities into the suburbs, taking many of the employment opportunities blacks needed into communities where they were not welcome to live."[50] The result of this trend was the formation and growth of ghettos, or areas of inner cities with high minority populations that were plagued by levels of high unemployment, poverty, and crime.

Disturbing Realities

In 1988 Congress passed the next piece of housing-related legislation, which was called the Fair Housing Amendments Act. Among its many provisions, the new legislation established that HUD was the designated government agency for enforcing the 1968 Fair Housing Act and for investigating complaints.

Today HUD conducts studies of geographic areas throughout

The Insidious Red Line

Today blatant housing discrimination is illegal under the Fair Housing Act, which was signed into law in 1968. But before that a practice known as redlining was common throughout the United States. Redlining refers to efforts that are intended to keep particular groups of people, typically minorities, from buying or renting in certain areas. It also describes efforts to cluster minorities in designated neighborhoods or parts of town.

The term *redlining* was coined in the 1960s by John McKnight, a sociologist and community development specialist from Ohio, who used it to describe a practice that was often used by banks. Bank officials drew red lines around certain geographic areas on maps to indicate where they were not willing to loan money for property, such as black neighborhoods in inner cities. In his book *Business Scandals, Corruption, and Reform*, author Gary Giroux writes, "One of the public policy problems of home ownership until the 1960s was the 'whites only' attitude even by federal agencies. Minorities also were separated from whites geographically, a practice called 'redlining.'"

Gary Giroux, *Business Scandals, Corruption, and Reform*. Santa Barbara, CA: Greenwood, 2013, p. 487.

the United States and prepares reports based on its findings. One of these reports, released in June 2013, revealed that even though blatant acts of housing-related discrimination continue to decline in the United States, more subtle forms are still a reality for home and apartment seekers. A key finding was that minority renters and potential home buyers are being told about and shown fewer homes and apartments than are whites with similar backgrounds. "Fewer minorities today may be getting the door slammed in their faces," says HUD secretary Shaun Donovan, "but we continue to see evidence of housing discrimination that can limit a family's housing, economic, and educational opportunities."[51]

The study was conducted with testers working in pairs, of whom one was white and the other was black, Hispanic, or Asian. Across twenty-eight metropolitan areas of the country, the pairs conducted more than eight thousand tests. This involved contacting a housing provider to inquire about a home or apartment randomly selected from those that had recently been advertised. Testers then independently recorded the treatment they experienced, including information about all homes and apartments recommended and shown to them during the study period. One particularly interesting finding was that Hispanics posing as potential home buyers were treated about the same as whites, whereas blacks and Asian Americans were treated differently and given fewer options for homes they might purchase. In terms of renting homes or apartments, though, whites received preferential treatment to all minorities.

"Fewer minorities today may be getting the door slammed in their faces, but we continue to see evidence of housing discrimination that can limit a family's housing, economic, and educational opportunities."[51]

— Shaun Donovan, secretary of HUD.

In one case, an agent told an Asian tester that a two-bedroom apartment was available as advertised but that no other units were available for rent. A white tester who met with the same agent just a few hours later was told about the availability of four other two-bedroom units in different locations. "That's typical of the kind of unequal treatment we observed across metropolitan housing markets nationwide," says Margery Turner, who is the Urban Institute's senior vice president for program planning and management. "It's fundamentally unfair somebody would get information about fewer homes and apartments just because of the color of their skin. But it also really raises the cost of housing search for minorities and it restricts the housing choices available to them."[52]

Other findings of the study involved black testers who posed as renters; they were told about 11.4 percent fewer units than their white counterparts and were shown 4.2 percent fewer units. Black testers who said they were interested in buying a home were told about 17 percent fewer homes and shown 17.7 percent fewer

A decades-old photograph captures scenes of New York City's Spanish Harlem neighborhood. Between the 1950s and 1980s many white Americans moved to suburbs, leaving poor blacks and others in inner city neighborhoods.

homes than were white testers. Hispanic testers were told about 12.5 percent fewer apartments for rent and shown 7.5 percent fewer. Asian testers were told about 9.8 percent fewer and shown 6.6 percent fewer apartments than their white counterparts.

An African American woman from New York City personally experienced what the HUD study revealed about housing discrimination. The woman, who is well educated and earns a very good income, has submitted numerous applications for apartments to no avail. She strongly suspects that this is happening because she is black "and it's easy to discern that from my name alone." She writes,

> I envision a scenario where my application is being considered next to a nonminority application and the powers that be choose the other applicants because they are per-

ceived to be less of a risk. I attended a top college and have previously paid rents as high as $1,575 a month in downtown Manhattan; I have no marks on my credit score, and I have a high-paying job at a top asset management firm on Wall Street. Race must be a factor that is in play here. I'm tired of seeing my dream apartments plucked out from under my nose because of factors that I can't control. . . . I'm truly running out of patience.[53]

Another Watchdog Group

The woman's complaint is one of thousands that are investigated each year by HUD and other agencies, one of which is the National Fair Housing Alliance (NFHA). A consortium of civil rights and fair housing groups and individuals, the NFHA is committed to helping US residents obtain equal access to housing. One of its tasks is to conduct national and regional investigations of policies and practices and then prepare reports of its findings. One of these, which was released in April 2012, is titled *Fair Housing in a Changing Nation*. The report makes it clear that housing discrimination still exists in the United States, and the country remains "highly segregated," as the authors write: "A conservative estimate puts the number of violations of fair housing law at four million every year. Many people do not know their rights under the Fair Housing Act, and of those who do, many do not report housing discrimination because they don't know where to go, they believe nothing will be done about it, or they fear the consequences."[54]

"A conservative estimate puts the number of violations of fair housing law at four million every year."[54]

— The NFHA, which investigates housing-related discrimination complaints.

The NFHA found that rental cases represented the bulk of the housing-related complaints. The agency says this is consistent with past investigations, and it is likely due to rental-related discrimination being easier to recognize when it happens. The NFHA report shows that there were 15,164 complaints of housing discrimination in the United States rental market during 2011, which was an increase over 2010 when complaints totaled 14,782. In the home sales market, the NFHA investigation revealed 302 complaints of discrimination,

The Hero of Fair Housing

In a blog post of October 25, 2013, public policy and civil rights advocate Nancy Amidei paid tribute to Edward Brooke, a man she refers to as the "hero of the affordable housing movement." Brooke, who was the first African American to be popularly elected to the US Senate, was a champion of fair housing legislation. When expressing his support for the law, he used his own experience as an example of why it was sorely needed. Brooke served with the US Army during World War II, earning both the Bronze Star and the distinguished service award—but disappointment and frustration awaited him upon returning home. He could not find a nice place for his family to live because landlords were unwilling to rent to black people.

When Brooke joined the Senate, he and Walter Mondale worked tirelessly to pass the Fair Housing Act, which was no easy task. "At the time, the Civil Rights Act was still new," says Amidei. "In much of the country, neighborhoods, schools, businesses, the military, and even churches were strictly segregated by race. And notions like 'equal employment' or 'fair housing' were instantly, viciously, fought." Finally their hard work paid off, and the Fair Housing Act became law in April 1968. Amidei writes, "Ed Brooke was one politician who made a difference."

Nancy Amidei, "Ed Brooke: Saluting a Housing Champion," *Washington Low Income Housing Alliance Blog*, October 28, 2013. www.wliha.org.

which was an improvement over the 441 complaints reported in 2010. Additionally, the NFHA report includes complaints of harassment. In 2011 the agency received 552 reports of harassment toward tenants, residents, or home seekers, and nearly 45 percent of these were based on race.

Another area of investigation for the NFHA is discrimination by banks and mortgage companies. In February 2014 the group announced that a formal housing discrimination complaint had been filed against Bank of America, one of the largest banks in the United States. An undercover investigation revealed that a bank branch in Charleston, South Carolina, was openly discriminating against Hispanic mortgage applicants. Over a period of several months, the NFHA sent Hispanic and white individuals to the bank posing as prospective borrowers. The Hispanics were presented as more qualified than the whites, with higher incomes, more money available for down payments and closing costs, and stronger employment profiles. It quickly became apparent that despite their superior qualifications, Hispanics were treated worse than their white counterparts.

In one instance, a white woman who was working undercover for the NFHA stopped at the Charleston bank branch and had a brief meeting with an employee, to whom she expressed interest in getting a home loan. The woman left the bank and almost immediately received a follow-up call from a loan officer who wanted to discuss her situation. He then emailed her multiple estimates for monthly payments and closing costs, offered the option of a bank credit to offset her closing costs, and provided contact information for two real estate agents. Several hours later a Hispanic woman (also working undercover) visited the same bank branch—and her experience was markedly different.

After expressing interest in getting a home loan, she was told by a bank employee that she would be contacted by a loan officer. The NFHA writes that "in contrast to the white individual, the Latina individual was never contacted."[55] Upon further investigation, the NFHA discovered that other housing-related complaints had also been filed against the Charleston bank. For instance, it failed to maintain the upkeep of foreclosed homes in predominantly minority neighborhoods in contrast to neighborhoods with mostly white residents.

Denver Discrimination Dilemma

Housing-related discrimination is prevalent throughout the United States, but some cities have a more difficult struggle with it than others. One of these cities is Denver, Colorado. In late 2013 an extensive audit by the Denver Metro Fair Housing Center revealed that discrimination in Denver's rental market is a serious problem. As with the HUD study, the 2013 Denver audit involved deploying pairs of testers: eleven whites paired with eleven Hispanics, and another twelve whites paired with twelve African Americans. The February 2014 final report explains the study results:

> The audit reveals not only the extent of housing discrimination in the Denver metro area, but also how discriminatory practices and policies are manifested in the rental industry. Although blatant discriminatory comments from housing providers are rare, rental agents and managers frequently discourage African Americans, Latinos, and families with children from applying through more subtle actions and statements, while encouraging white housing seekers or those without children to apply. One of the most common types of differential treatment encountered in the audit involved housing providers misrepresenting the number of units actually available to people of color or individuals with children. These practices are prohibited by federal and Colorado fair housing laws.[56]

Some specific findings of the audit included the discovery that 67 percent of the time white testers were treated more favorably by housing providers than African American testers—and 91 percent of the time white testers were treated better than their Hispanic counterparts. Also, less information about available rental housing was provided to African American testers than to whites. One example was that of a black tester who was never told that if she put down a deposit, the unit would be held for her; her white counterpart was asked by the same agent if she wanted to put down a deposit that day to hold the unit. "Additionally," the report states, "the white tester was told by this agent that she thought she would fit in well at the building but that the agent "could not say more because of fair housing."[57]

A number of people were surprised by the extent of the problem revealed by the report, including Pat Coyle, who directs the

An NAACP sign posted some years ago in a neighborhood of Atlanta, Georgia, seems to express the views of many people, even today, that progress has been made in eliminating racism but more work remains.

Colorado Division of Housing. "This has not been what we've seen as typical of the Denver marketplace," says Coyle. She adds that the audit findings will certainly be examined "in depth" to evaluate the severity of discrimination in the city. "We have to dig deeper into the causes,"[58] says Coyle.

Lingering Problems

Throughout the United States, housing discrimination has markedly diminished over the past fifty years, but by no means has it disappeared. Investigations by HUD, the NHFA, and other federal, state, and regional agencies continue to find a high prevalence of discrimination against minorities who are seeking to buy or rent places to live. The bad news is that these agencies are discovering serious problems in housing discrimination. But there is good news too: by bringing these problems to the public's attention, it puts pressure on people in the housing market to stop breaking the law.

Facts

- A June 2013 report by the HUD found that in the city of Atlanta, Georgia, nearly three times as many white people were offered two-year leases compared with black apartment hunters.

- A lawsuit filed in August 2012 against Winchester, Connecticut, claims that city officials discriminate against minorities in how they administer a federal housing subsidy program, thus ensuring that the population will remain overwhelmingly white.

- According to the Leadership Conference on Civil and Human Rights, white home buyers received 98 percent of loans approved by the federal government between 1934 and 1968.

- An April 2012 report by the NFHA states that African Americans, regardless of income, are highly likely to live in poor neighborhoods over the course of a decade, while only 10 percent of whites are expected to do the same.

- In January 2014 the US Department of Justice settled a lawsuit in which persons of Middle Eastern and South Asian ancestry were discriminated against at an apartment complex in Euless, Texas.

Are Affirmative Action Programs Justified?

CHAPTER FOUR

When asked the question of whether African Americans were harmed in the past by the effects of racism, few people could truthfully answer no. Historical records make it clear that white Americans considered themselves superior to blacks from the time the country was founded, and that attitude prevailed for centuries. It was not until the mid-1960s that civil rights legislation launched an antidiscrimination movement in the United States. Because African Americans had been downtrodden for so long, they severely lagged behind whites in terms of education and employment. As a way of remedying this problem, and giving minorities a boost to help them catch up to their white peers, a concept known as affirmative action came into being. On June 4, 1965, President Lyndon B. Johnson explained the importance of such a measure: "This is the next and the more profound stage of the battle for civil rights. We seek not just freedom, but opportunity."[59]

"This is the next and the more profound stage of the battle for civil rights. We seek not just freedom, but opportunity."[59]

— Lyndon B. Johnson, the thirty-sixth president of the United States.

Attempting to Bridge the Gap

It was actually Johnson's predecessor, John F. Kennedy, who was first to coin the term *affirmative action* and champion the cause.

On March 6, 1961, Kennedy signed Executive Order 10925, which directed government contractors to take "affirmative action to ensure that applicants are employed, and employees are treated during employment, without regard to their race, creed, color, or national origin."[60] Kennedy's intent in signing this executive order was to assert the government's commitment to equal opportunity for all, and to take action to make that commitment become reality, rather than simply words on paper.

Because Johnson shared Kennedy's passion about affirmative action, he advanced the cause in 1965 by signing his own executive order. At the time, even though civil rights legislation had improved employment and education opportunities for African Americans, they still lagged significantly behind whites. According

States That Say No to Affirmative Action

As of June 2014 eight US states had affirmative action bans in place. The first state to enact such legislation was California, where voters approved Resolution SP-1 in July 1995. The law eliminated any consideration of race, ethnicity, and gender in admission decisions for schools in the University of California system. The state later extended the ban to cover all public education, public employment, and public contracting. In 1998 the state of Washington passed similar legislation, as did Florida in 1999. Texas banned affirmative action in 1997, but the law was later overturned.

The twenty-first century saw five states pass anti–affirmative action laws: Michigan in 2006, Nebraska in 2008, Arizona in 2010, New Hampshire in 2011, and Oklahoma in 2012. In Colorado, Amendment 46 would have prohibited affirmative action in public education, employment, and public contracting, but voters defeated the bill in November 2008.

to the National Conference of State Legislatures, in 1965 only 5 percent of undergraduate college students, 1 percent of law students, and 2 percent of medical students in the United States were black. Research also showed that qualified black applicants were much less likely to be hired for jobs than their white counterparts. When they were employed, blacks were regularly passed over for promotions and salary increases compared with white employees in similar positions.

Affirmative Action at Work

The racial makeup of America's workforce has changed dramatically since the 1960s, with far greater diversity today. The term *affirmative action* is defined much the same as it was years ago: the implementation of policies that give an edge to people who have suffered from discrimination, particularly in employment and education. Those who support such policies emphasize that they are necessary to level the playing field for people who still face many race-related hurdles. Included among the supporters are some of America's largest and most successful corporations. In a 2012 document, executives from more than fifty top US companies formally expressed their support for affirmative action programs. These companies included Xerox, Aetna, General Electric, Pepsi, Kraft, IBM, Shell Oil, Procter and Gamble, Gap Inc., Dow Chemical, Kodak, and Wal-Mart, among others.

The corporations stress in the document how their own experience has shown that "a workforce trained in a diverse environment is critical to their business success." They emphasize a strong commitment to diversity as a key part of their business, culture, and planning, but they also make it clear that they cannot reach this diversity goal on their own. For that, corporate leaders depend on colleges and universities to recruit and teach "qualified minority candidates and create an environment in which all students can meaningfully expand their horizons."[61]

People who have been educated in a diverse setting benefit from the experience as do their employers. Corporate executives say these employees are better equipped to work with coworkers, business partners, and clients from around the world. In the

An ethnically diverse group works together on a project. Many large companies support continued use of affirmative action policies to ensure diverse workplaces, which are considered essential to business success.

2012 document the corporate executives state that such employees are likely to help foster "a more positive work environment by decreasing incidents of discrimination and stereotyping." The overall message being emphasized by corporate leaders is that affirmative action programs result in the kind of diversity that is crucial for businesses to succeed in today's "challenging economic environment."[62]

Two Success Stories

World-renowned neurosurgeon Ben Carson is an example of how affirmative action can help someone become extraordinarily successful. Carson, who is African American, says that when he was a child growing up in Detroit and Boston he "had many opportunities to experience the ugly face of racism and witnessed the devastating toll exacted by its mean-spirited nature." He explains what affirmative action was intended to do, saying it was "based on the admirable concept that we should take into consideration inherent difficulties faced by minorities growing up in a racist society."[63]

An affirmative action policy at prestigious Yale University helped Carson get an excellent undergraduate education, which he followed by graduating from the University of Michigan Medical School. "Medical school was transformative," he says, "and I was subsequently accepted into the selective neurosurgical residency at Johns Hopkins. By that time, no special considerations were expected or needed."[64] In other words, Carson was given a helping hand through affirmative action. Once he was on his way up the medical career ladder, he was expected to be able to climb the rest of the way on his own.

Berneta Hayes also benefited from affirmative action, and she is on her way to becoming a lawyer. Now a student at the University of Iowa College of Law, Hayes cannot say enough about how important this advantage has been to her. "I'm not ashamed to admit that without affirmative action, I'm not certain I would be on the precipice of the law career that I'm at right now," she says. "As an African-American woman from a poor family, I have little doubt that affirmative action helped me get into college, earn a degree, and enroll in law school."[65]

When Hayes was a freshman at Drury University in Springfield, Missouri, she was often the only black student in her classes. Invariably the subject of affirmative action would come up, and during one classroom discussion several white students made it clear that they had no such advantages when they applied for admission. "One even suggested that I probably grew up with more privileges than some of the white students," she says, "so I did not deserve 'special treatment' over them."[66] Hayes explained how very wrong they were about her background and assured them that, being white, they had an innate advantage that had never been available to her.

"As an African-American woman from a poor family, I have little doubt that affirmative action helped me get into college, earn a degree, and enroll in law school."[65]

— Aspiring lawyer Berneta Hayes.

The Backlash

Hayes was pleased to find that her classmates were open to what she had to say, and it led to an enlightening discussion. It is not uncommon for such disagreements to erupt instead into contentious arguments because affirmative action is a highly controversial issue. One of the main objections is that such policies unfairly discriminate against whites, which is often called reverse discrimination. This term arose during the 1970s, with the first lawsuit that formally challenged affirmative action.

At the time the concept was still relatively new, and colleges and universities were adopting policies to attract and retain a more diverse student body. One tactic used by some schools was reserving a certain number of places each year specifically for minorities, which was the case with the medical school of the University of California, Davis (UCD). The school adopted an admissions policy in which sixteen out of one hundred places in each class were reserved for minority students. Although UCD officials had honorable intentions when they enacted this affirmative action policy,

Unsubstantiated Claims

On May 18, 1998, Robert Farmer filed a lawsuit against the University of Maryland School of Medicine. Farmer had twice applied for admission and was rejected both times, which he claimed was because of the school's affirmative action policy. Specifically, he alleged that the university had "drastically lower standards for the admission of members of certain favored minority groups, especially blacks." Farmer further claimed that his test scores and grades were higher than those of accepted black students. By the time he filed the lawsuit, Farmer was already a student at a medical school in the Netherlands. One of his complaints in the suit was that he had been forced into attending an inferior foreign medical school.

In 2001 a federal judge dismissed the case. He made it clear that the reason Farmer's application had been rejected was not due to his race. Rather, his academic qualifications fell short of the medical school's requirements.

Quoted in Leagle, Inc., "*Farmer v. Ramsay*," August 15, 2001. www.leagle.com.

it landed them in court facing a reverse-discrimination lawsuit.

The suit was filed by a white man named Allan Bakke, a former military officer who was an engineer with the National Aeronautics and Space Administration (NASA). In 1973 Bakke was rejected after applying to the UCD medical school, and the same thing happened when he applied again the following year. This occurred even though Bakke's academic qualifications and test scores were better than several African American students who were accepted to the school. Convinced that he was being discriminated against, Bakke filed a lawsuit with the Superior Court of California in June 1974. The court sided with him, the university appealed the decision, and the case went before the US Supreme Court in 1978.

> "Racial and ethnic classifications of any sort are inherently suspect and call for the most exacting judicial scrutiny."[67]
>
> — Supreme Court justice Lewis F. Powell.

In June 1978 the Court ruled in favor of Bakke, stating that UCD officials could no longer reserve a set number of places specifically for nonwhite students. By doing so, the justices explained, the school was in violation of the US Constitution's Fourteenth Amendment, which guarantees all Americans equal protection under the law. Thus, the school's rigid quota policies were unconstitutional. Justice Lewis F. Powell wrote,

> Racial and ethnic classifications of any sort are inherently suspect and call for the most exacting judicial scrutiny. While the goal of achieving a diverse student body is sufficiently compelling to justify consideration of race in admissions decisions under some circumstances, petitioner's special admissions program, which forecloses consideration to persons like respondent, is unnecessary to the achievement of this compelling goal, and therefore invalid under the [Constitution's] Equal Protection Clause.[67]

Although the ruling mandated changes in how the school went about its admissions process, the justices did not outlaw affirmative action altogether. Rather, they clarified that when students apply to the university, their race may be one of many considerations that help foster diversity—but race may not be the sole factor for making decisions about admission.

Abigail Fisher contended she was denied admission to the University of Texas because she is white. The US Supreme Court, which ruled on the case in 2013, did not outlaw affirmative action programs but said they cannot be the sole tool for achieving racial diversity on college campuses.

Rejected and Resentful

In the more than three decades since the *Bakke* ruling, affirmative action has continued to be a topic of heated debate. Some who oppose it are offended by the idea that race is still a factor at all in a university's admissions policy. They are convinced that the Supreme Court's landmark 1978 decision did not go far enough; by not outlawing affirmative action, the court clearly left the door open for reverse discrimination against white students. This was the allegation of a young white woman named Abigail Fisher. In 2008 Fisher applied to the University of Texas (UT) and was denied admission. The university's policy was to automatically accept students who place in the top 10 percent of their high school graduating class, and Fisher did not meet that qualification. Additional students were considered for admission to UT based on a group of factors, including grade-point average (GPA), talents, leadership qualities, family circumstances, and race. Fisher placed in the top

12 percent of her class in Austin, Texas, was involved in extracurricular activities, and carried a 3.59 GPA. She became convinced that if race had not been a consideration she would have been accepted by the university. Claiming that she had been a victim of racial discrimination Fisher sued UT in US district court in 2008. The following year the court upheld UT's admissions policy and dismissed Fisher's case. Her attorney promptly petitioned for it to go before the US Supreme Court, which the court granted.

On June 24, 2013, the justices issued their ruling. Although they did not outlaw affirmative action, a majority concluded that such programs must meet strict criteria. For instance, a college or university cannot simply use affirmative action as a way of achieving racial diversity. Race may be used as a criterion only if necessary, meaning there is no other realistic alternative to achieve a diverse student body. Because the appeals court had not examined this carefully enough, the Supreme Court sent Fisher's case back to the lower court for further consideration. Fisher considered this decision a victory even though she did not actually win her case. "I'm grateful to the justices," she says, "for moving the nation closer to a day when students' race isn't used at all in college admissions."[68]

What Americans Think

Soon after the Supreme Court announced its ruling on the *Fisher* case, the research group Gallup conducted a survey to determine the public's opinions about affirmative action. More than forty-three hundred adults living in the United States took part in the survey, including Caucasians, African Americans, and Hispanics. When asked whether they thought race should be a factor in college admissions or whether students should be admitted solely on merit, 67 percent said merit, and 28 percent believed that race should also be considered. Interestingly, however, most participants said they support affirmative action programs. Although it seems contradictory, when asked whether they generally favor or oppose such programs for racial minorities, 58 percent said they were in favor of the programs and 37 percent opposed them. Gallup's Jeffrey M. Jones shares his thoughts:

Americans are not averse to having the government take steps to help improve the conditions of minority groups in the United States, and in a broad sense express support for affirmative action programs. One of the clearest examples of affirmative action in practice is colleges' taking into account a person's racial or ethnic background when deciding which applicants will be admitted. Americans seem reluctant to endorse such a practice, and even blacks, who have historically been helped by such programs, are divided on the matter.[69]

Another poll was conducted between May 30 and June 2, 2013, by NBC News and the *Wall Street Journal*. This poll, which involved one thousand adults, was also intended to gauge public opinion about affirmative action. Drawing comparisons with similar surveys conducted since 1991, researchers found that there had been a steady decline in the number of Americans who support affirmative action. In 1991, for instance, when asked if the program was still needed or should be ended, 61 percent of participants said it was still needed. By the time the later poll was conducted, the number of Americans supporting affirmative action had dropped to 45 percent.

The Concept of Mismatch

Two experts who are not at all surprised at the decline in public support for affirmative action are economist and University of California, Los Angeles (UCLA), law professor Richard Sander and Brookings Institution senior fellow Stuart Taylor Jr. They acknowledge that the idea grew out of the best of intentions: a "noble effort to jump-start racial integration and foster equal opportunity." But, they argue, "somewhere along the decades, it has lost its way. Over time, it has become a political lightning rod and one of our most divisive social policies."[70]

Sander and Taylor do not necessarily think that affirmative action is a bad concept. Rather, their issue is that it has led to a phenomenon they term *mismatch,* whereby the programs that are intended to benefit minorities actually harm them. Mismatch, ac-

Supporters of affirmative action rally outside the US Supreme Court Building in 2012. Americans generally support diversity in colleges and the workplace but have mixed views on the use of affirmative action programs to achieve that goal.

cording to Sander and Taylor, results when a school gives minority students such preferential treatment (because of factors such as race and/or athletic ability) that they end up in classes for which they are not academically prepared compared with their peers. Either the classes move along too fast for them to keep up or they require background knowledge that these students have not obtained. Sander and Taylor explain:

> The student who would flourish at, say, Wake Forest or the University of Richmond, instead finds himself at Duke, where the professors are not teaching at a pace designed for him—they are teaching to the "middle" of the class, introducing terms and concepts at a speed that is unnerving even to the best-prepared student. The student who is underprepared relative to others in that class falls behind from the start and becomes increasingly lost as the professor and his classmates race ahead. His grades on his first exams or papers put him at the bottom of the class. Worse, the experience may well induce panic and self-doubt, making learning even harder.[71]

According to Sander and Taylor, mismatch holds the answer to a perplexing phenomenon: even though black students are just as likely, or even more likely, to enter college than are white students with similar backgrounds, the black students usually get lower grades, rank toward the bottom of the class, and drop out far more often than whites. Sander and Taylor write, "Because of mismatch, racial preference policies often stigmatize minorities, reinforce pernicious stereotypes, and undermine the self-confidence of beneficiaries, rather than creating the diverse racial utopias so often advertised in college campus brochures."[72]

Not everyone agrees about the mismatch theory. Even some who do acknowledge that it is troubling argue that the problem is not nearly as severe as Sander and Taylor claim. Two opponents of the theory are Richard A. Berk, a professor of criminology and statistics at the University of Pennsylvania, and Daniel E. Ho, a law professor at Stanford University. Another noted professional who spoke out against the mismatch concept was the late Theodore Eisenberg, a professor at Cornell University School of Law and a noted civil rights pioneer. Before his death in February 2014, Eisenberg shared his thoughts about mismatch with journalist Dan Slater. "Mismatch angers affirmative-action supporters because it quantifies a downside without weighing it against potential upsides," Eisenberg said, "such as the benefit of a diverse classroom, and the reality that some people who do attend better schools because of affirmative action are more successful in life as a result and help other minorities thrive."[73]

Can This Be Resolved?

Affirmative action was once touted as the answer to solving America's problem of racial segregation and inequality in education and employment. Although many people still believe the program has merit and should continue, surveys show that its popularity has significantly waned over the years. People who support affirmative action believe that if minority students are not given some sort of an edge, they will never be able to catch up with their white peers. Those who are against it acknowledge that it may have been a good concept in the past, but now it is no longer necessary. A common objection is that affirmative action policies result in reverse discrimination that unfairly hurts white people. In the coming years, there will undoubtedly be more challenges to affirmative action, and what the courts decide may determine, once and for all, what its fate will be.

Facts

- **In a May–June 2013 poll cosponsored by NBC News and the *Wall Street Journal*, 45 percent of participants said they believed affirmative action programs are still needed; an equal 45 percent said they feel affirmative action programs unfairly discriminate against whites.**

- **Since the use of affirmative action was banned in California's public university admissions processes, the rate of black and Hispanic students has dropped from 21 percent to 18 percent, and Asian American students now dominate admissions.**

- **According to a June 2013 *New York Times* story, the University of Florida and Florida State University have been more successful than colleges in other states at maintaining minority student enrollment despite a ban on affirmative action.**

- **According to UCLA law professor Richard Sander and economist Stuart Taylor Jr., academic struggle results when minority students who got Bs in high school are put into competition with Asian and white students who got As in high school.**

- **According to the social change group Do Something, although research findings vary, affirmative action in college admissions is the equivalent of adding 150 to 310 points on an SAT college admissions test score for a minority student.**

CHAPTER FIVE

What Progress Has Been Made in the Fight Against Racism?

Although its severity is often debated, racism is still an everyday reality for people of color. It is not as blatant as in the past; rather, the racism of today is often revealed in extremely subtle ways. Says Terrance Heath, an online producer and writer for the Campaign for America's Future in Washington, DC, "Its nature can be interpersonal or institutional. It doesn't always carry a sign, wave a confederate battle flag, or carry handcuffs. It may not even be consciously intended. It can be hard to pin down, and next to impossible to prove. . . . None of that makes the impact any less real."[74]

A Child Victim

What Heath has described is very familiar to Eadie Harley, a Michigan woman who has a three-year-old biracial granddaughter. "This child looks like a miniature version of Halle Berry," says Harley. "She's beautiful, with café au lait skin and Shirley Temple hair, and she's sweet, and funny, and charming. And the reality is, there are people out there who look at her like they hate her even though she's just an innocent little girl. You can see it in their eyes. And when it happens it's so devastating I feel physically ill."[75]

On one particular occasion Harley took her granddaughter, whose name is Makenna, out to lunch at a restaurant. A man and woman were seated in an adjacent booth, and Harley happened to glance over at them. "They were glaring at me and their faces were like stone," she says. Thinking she had perhaps misunderstood, Harley smiled at the couple—and immediately knew she had assessed them correctly. "The woman actually sneered at me," says Harley. "She narrowed her eyes and looked at Makenna, then at me, then back at Makenna, and the only way to describe the look on her face is disgust. That anyone could feel that way about this beautiful child . . . it is just inconceivable." Although Makenna is still too young to understand the concept of racism, Harley is fearful about what the child will face in the future. "I can protect her now," she says, "because she's still tiny. But there will come a time when I won't be able to protect her from it anymore, and that's heartbreaking. It hurts so much I can't even think about it."[76]

A Civil Rights Trailblazer

What Harley describes is an unfortunate reminder that racism is still alive and well in the United States. But progress has been made in the fight against it, which is largely due to the courageous people who fought discrimination and segregation years ago. Of course these heroes of the past include the man known as the father of the civil rights movement, Martin Luther King Jr., who was fiercely devoted to achieving racial equality. Another hero in the fight against racism was a black woman from Montgomery, Alabama, named Rosa Parks. She, too, is remembered for her courage and willingness to put herself at risk in order to right a wrong. For that, she became known as the mother of the civil rights movement—although the incident that made her famous occurred simply because she was exhausted and needed to sit down.

> "I didn't feel very good about being told to stand up and not have a seat. I felt I had a right to stay where I was."[77]
>
> — The renowned civil rights activist Rosa Parks, speaking about her refusal to give up her seat on a bus to a white man in 1955.

On the evening of December 1, 1955, all Parks wanted was to get home after a long day working as a seamstress. She boarded a bus and walked past the first rows of seats, which were reserved for white pas-

A police officer fingerprints Rosa Parks after she refused to move to the back of the bus in a now-famous 1955 incident in Montgomery, Alabama. Parks has said she stayed put because she was, quite simply, exhausted but her action led to a long-running bus boycott.

sengers only. Parks chose a seat near the middle of the bus, in the first row of the "colored" section. Three other black people were seated in the same row. They rode without incident until the third stop, when a small group of whites boarded the bus. Because there were not enough seats in the front section, one white man was left standing in the aisle. The bus driver told Parks and the other black passengers that that they would have to move to make room for the white man to sit. The three complied—but Parks did not. She refused to give up her seat, as she explained during an interview many years later: "I didn't feel very good about being told to stand up and not have a seat. I felt I had a right to stay where I was. That was why I told the driver I was not going to stand."[77]

Soon after Parks made it clear that she was staying in her seat, two police officers boarded the bus and the driver told them about Parks's refusal to follow his order. "The policeman walked down and asked me why I didn't stand up," Parks said, "and I said I didn't think I should stand up. 'Why do you push us around?' I asked him. And he said, 'I don't know. But the law is the law and you are under arrest.' As soon as he said that I stood up, [and] the three of us left the bus together." The officers drove Parks to the police station, where she was fingerprinted, booked, and locked in a jail cell. "I didn't feel good about going to jail," she said, "but I was willing to go to let it be known that under this type of segregation, black people had endured too much for too long."[78]

Parks placed a telephone call to Edgar D. Nixon, a prominent civil rights leader whom she had come to know through her involvement with the NAACP. Nixon bailed Parks out of jail and took her home. She was later convicted of violating a city law requiring segregation of public buses, and Nixon filed an appeal on her behalf. News of her arrest and conviction traveled fast in the African American community. Parks was highly respected and well liked. One black woman exclaimed upon hearing what happened, "They've messed with the wrong one now."[79] Because of how people felt about Parks, they had no hesitation about standing up for her—and at the same time, finally speaking out against the discriminatory practice of segregation.

The group organized and carried out a massive bus boycott. Suddenly, forty thousand black people stopped riding buses in Montgomery. This was a huge economic hardship for the busing company since African Americans made up at least 75 percent of total bus ridership. The black people of Montgomery got their message across. After dragging on for more than a year (381 days), the bus boycott finally came to an end on December 21, 1956. The US Supreme Court had ruled that the segregation law was unconstitutional, and all buses in Montgomery were integrated. Black people once again began riding buses—but no longer were they told where they had to sit.

Landmark Legislation

Between December 1956, when the Montgomery bus boycott ended, and the early 1960s, very little was done to further the civil rights cause. The US Congress established a civil rights section of the US Department of Justice as well as a Commission on Civil Rights that was charged with investigating complaints of discrimination. Then, in June 1963, John F. Kennedy proposed comprehensive civil rights legislation, saying that the United States "will

A Brave and Admirable Woman

Rosa Parks was born Rosa Louise McCauley in 1913 in Tuskegee, Alabama. As a child she moved to the town of Pine Level, near Montgomery. She was at first homeschooled by her mother, then she attended segregated schools, and later she had to drop out of high school before graduating to care for ill family members. At the age of nineteen she met and married her husband, Raymond Parks, who was active in the Montgomery chapter of the NAACP. She completed her high school diploma and then joined the NAACP, where she served as youth leader and secretary to the president.

Parks's refusal in 1955 to give her seat on a segregated bus to a white man led to her arrest and the successful boycott of the Montgomery buses. This became a pivotal event in the civil rights movement, and Parks became a renowned civil rights activist. In 1965 she was hired by US Representative John Conyers, for whom she worked until her retirement. In 1996 President Bill Clinton awarded Parks the Presidential Medal of Freedom, and in 1999 the US Congress awarded her its highest honor, the Congressional Gold Medal. Parks died in 2005 at the age of ninety-two. In 2013 she was honored posthumously when President Barack Obama unveiled a statue of her in the US Capitol.

not be fully free until all of its citizens are free."[80] The following November, after Kennedy's tragic and untimely death, Lyndon B. Johnson assumed the office of president. As passionate and committed as Kennedy had been, Johnson continued moving the civil rights cause forward.

On July 2, 1964, after a long and difficult struggle with Congress, Johnson signed into law the Civil Rights Act of 1964. It banned segregation on the grounds of race, religion, or national origin at all public places, including courthouses, parks, restaurants, theaters, sports arenas, and hotels. Referring to the law as "one of the crowning legislative achievements of the civil rights movement," a History.com documentary explains that "no longer could blacks and other minorities be denied service simply based on the color of their skin. The act also barred race, religious, national origin and gender discrimination by employers and labor unions, and created an Equal Employment Opportunity Commission with the power to file lawsuits on behalf of aggrieved workers."[81]

The Civil Rights Act laid the groundwork for a package of laws that expanded and protected the rights of African Americans. For example, it paved the way for the Voting Rights Act of 1965, which outlawed literacy tests and other discriminatory tactics that discouraged black people from voting, and the 1968 Fair Housing Act. "Though the struggle against racism would continue," says History.com, "legal segregation had been brought to its knees."[82]

Breaking the Silence

More than four decades have passed since the civil rights movement was in full swing, and a great deal has changed over that time. Because of that, some people are under the impression that racism is no longer a serious problem. They argue, therefore, that it should not be a frequent topic of discussion because that perpetuates the issue and creates a problem. This is the perspective of John Hawkins, a white conservative commentator who created the Right Wing News site. Hawkins contends that people are "hypersensitive" about racism. "Keep in mind," he says,

> that we live in a nation with a black President and a black Attorney General. Furthermore, the government is legally allowed to discriminate against white Americans based on the color of their skin and it happily does so; yet you can't go a day in this country without hearing liberals howling about what a racist country they live in. It has almost become a circular, faith-based argument. America is racist because so many liberals say it's racist because they've heard other liberals say the country is racist.[83]

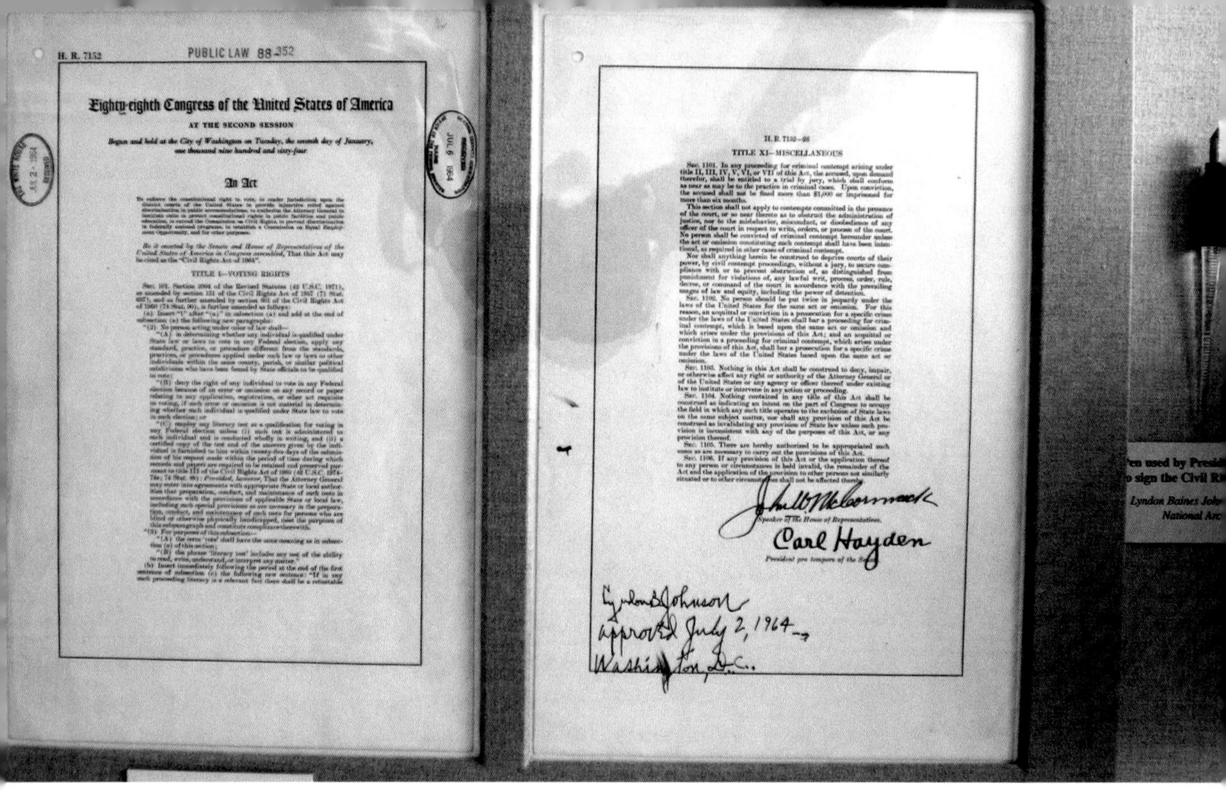

The Civil Rights Act, signed into law in 1964 by President Lyndon Johnson, is displayed at the White House in Washington, DC. The landmark law banned segregation on the grounds of race, religion, or national origin at all public places.

As a black man who has seen and experienced the effects of racism for his entire life, Terrance Heath has very little patience with people who claim that it is no longer a problem. "Black people don't have the luxury of pretending that racism is 'over,' even for a minute," he says. "Every week there's some fresh reminder that it's far from over." Heath is insistent that the only way to make progress toward ending racism is to keep the topic alive through communication; bringing it out in the open so people can better understand each other and talk about their differences. He writes,

> America has come a long way on the issue of race since Rosa Parks refused to give up her bus seat. We have come this far precisely because we have *not* stopped thinking about and talking about the reality of racism, and its impact on the lives of generations of Americans. We will not make further progress if we *stop* talking about it and stop thinking about it. We will lose ground. Racism will not magically "end" or disappear. It will merely go unchallenged. And those who defend it, justify it, or embed it in

their politics and ideology will get off the hook. We can't afford to let that happen.[84]

Comedian and writer Baratunde Thurston, who is also black, has a perspective similar to Heath's: that people need to bring racism out into the open so they can work on getting rid of it. In September 2013 Thurston blogged about an e-mail he had received from a white man who had read *How to Be Black*, a humorous memoir by Thurston that was published in 2012. The man loved the book and said it inspired him to do more to help create a racially equitable world. He wrote to Thurston asking for suggestions for how to go about that. Others had written for the same reason, so Thurston decided to compile a list of ideas (his own and from others) about what white people could do to help fight racism.

The first was, "Don't tolerate racism in your life. Call people out if they are being insensitive." Thurston expands on this, saying that if friends or acquaintances make racist or culturally insensitive remarks, people should not hesitate to speak up about it. "This can be done with sensitivity," says Thurston, "so that they don't simply feel attacked; it's a teachable moment."[85]

Student on a Mission

Teaching was exactly what Sy Stokes had in mind when he created a video called *The Black Bruins* in 2013. Stokes, who is a black college student, came up with the concept after being frustrated over his experience at UCLA. When he first arrived on campus as a freshman, Stokes was excited about joining a school that he had been told was diverse and welcoming to all kinds of people. Not long after he started classes, though, he became aware that the claim was not true. As an African American male, he felt isolated on a campus where only about 4 percent of students are black. Even though the school held regular debates about race, Stokes felt like the perspective of black male students was missing. So, he came up with the idea of the video. It features Stokes as the narrator, flanked by fellow black students holding signs with some statistics. Of men at UCLA,

"Black people don't have the luxury of pretending that racism is 'over,' even for a minute."[84]

—Terrance Heath, an online producer and blogger at Campaign for America's Future.

for instance, black males compose just 3.3 percent; of the 2,418 male students entering the school during the fall of 2013, only 48 of them were black. The video ends with Stokes and the others pulling off their UCLA sweatshirts, under which they are wearing plain black T-shirts.

Stokes posted his video on YouTube and soon had tens of thousands of views. The reactions were mixed, with many students who were critical and others who expressed support. No matter what is said about the video, Stokes is enthusiastic about the large response. "People are talking about the issue," he says, "and that's what counts."[86]

Taking a Stand Against Racism

Sociologists and others who study racism agree that talking about it is an important step toward eliminating it. And according to a July 2013 Rasmussen Reports survey, the majority of Americans believe that these sorts of conversations can happen. When asked if it is possible for people of different races in America to have open, honest discussions about racial issues, 64 percent of respondents said yes, they believe it is possible.

One organization that is devoted to fostering race-related discussions is the YWCA. Dara P. Richardson-Heron, a physician who is the chief executive officer of YWCA USA, says that bringing racism out into the open is crucial because it remains a serious problem. "In my opinion not much has changed with regard to racism in the recent past," she says. "You only have to turn on the television, look at the most recent 'apology' for a racial slur online or read the newspaper to see that racism is present everywhere."[87] One of the YWCA's antiracism programs is called Stand Against Racism. Organizations across the United States are invited to become participating sites by hosting their own "Stand," which is a private or public event where participants gather to take a pledge that they will stand up and fight racism. This powerful movement can potentially unite hundreds of thousands of dedicated people who, together, can make a positive difference toward fighting racism.

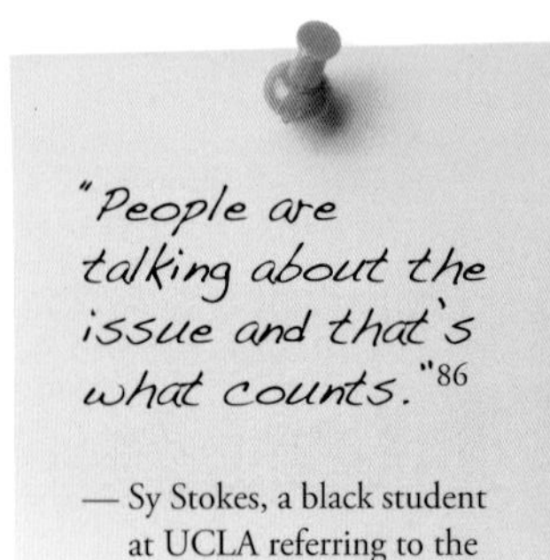

A White Man on Racism

Kevin A. Thompson is the lead pastor at a church in Fort Smith, Arkansas, and he has a ready answer if asked what a white man knows about racism. "Nothing," Thompson says. "That's what a white man knows about racism." Thompson goes on to say that of course he has heard about racism and may know a few facts that he learned; but only those who have personally experienced racism can truly understand it. Because Thompson is white, and was not raised in a racist family, he was under the impression that racism did not exist in Fort Smith. Now, after asking lots of questions, he realizes that racism was present "in ways I never imagined." He explains:

> When I hear the word "police," my first two thoughts are "They protect me" and "They were a good band." It doesn't cross my mind that they could profile me or be scared of me or do me harm.
>
> When something doesn't go my way, I might think someone has it out for me, but it never crosses my mind it could be because of the color of my skin.
>
> Even when I experience a person who does not like me because of the color of my skin, it is just an isolated incident and I have enough opportunities that it cannot define me.

Thompson concludes with a provocative statement: "I don't know racism and if you are white, neither do you."

Kevin A. Thompson, "What a White Man Knows About Racism," *KevinAThompson.com* (blog), January 19, 2014. www.kevinathompson.com.

Each year on the last Friday of April, many YWCAs host Stand Against Racism events. According to Richardson-Heron, 267,000 people and seventy-one local YWCAs participated in Stand Against

Newspapers in 2014 reported on racist statements made by Donald Sterling, the owner of the Los Angeles Clippers. Public figures are frequently caught on television or in social media making comments that are considered by many to be racial slurs.

Racism events in 2011. In 2012, the number was even higher: 311,500 people participated. Richardson-Heron says that these and other events sponsored by the YWCA are helping to expand awareness of racism, which is extremely important because it is still a serious problem—and many people still deny that. As she explains, "While I wish things were different . . . despite the tremendous work that has been done by iconic organizations like the YWCA over the past 154 years, it is still quite clear that racism in the U.S. is alive and well. . . . The first step in moving forward will be for everyone to be honest with themselves and admit that racism really does still exist . . . in a BIG way."[88] Richardson-Heron says that a primary goal of all YWCA race-related programs is to increase awareness, build trust, break down stereotypes and communication barriers, and build mutual respect and understanding of racial differences.

The Courage to Converse

These sorts of goals are also the focus of a program called Courageous Conversations About Race, which was created by Pacific Education Group founder and chief executive officer Glenn Singleton. The program is designed to foster discussions about racism to help people work toward eliminating it and is used by schools throughout the United States. Singleton is convinced that addressing racial inequalities will lead to a "more productive, efficient, and higher achieving" school system for students. "There are thousands of school districts across the country with these racial disparities that need to be addressed," he says. "It's becoming more difficult to ignore the elephant in the room—race matters."[89]

"There are thousands of school districts across the country with these racial disparities that need to be addressed."[89]

— Glenn Singleton, founder and chief executive officer of the Pacific Education Group.

The focus of Courageous Conversations is to help educators better understand issues that are unique to minority students. For instance, teachers learn how to conduct meaningful discussions in their classrooms during which students of all races learn from each other. Specific protocol for these conversations includes staying engaged in discussion, speaking the truth, being prepared to experience discomfort, and expecting/accepting that there will not necessarily be a resolution. Educators use a "compass" as their guide, which helps them learn more about how each person processes information about race. The compass visually helps students better understand one another's opinions and beliefs. "When we begin to surface those beliefs," says Singleton, "we can determine which of those beliefs are getting in the way of the [ideal] outcome where there's no racial disparity."[90]

Looking Ahead

An extraordinary amount of progress has been made since Rosa Parks bravely stood her ground on the Montgomery, Alabama, bus all those years ago. Thanks to her, along with tens of thousands of other dedicated individuals, segregation was outlawed in the late 1950s. During the following decade landmark civil rights legislation took effect, and the lives of people of color throughout the United States began to change for the better. Yet today, more than half a century later, racism in one form or another is still very much in existence. If people become aware of that, and embrace it as a worthwhile cause, that could be a promising first step toward getting rid of racism forever.

Facts

- **In a November 2013 poll commissioned by the Episcopal Church, eight out of ten participants agreed that in the future, Americans will be more accepting of all races.**

- **In September 2013 researchers from the University of Rochester released a study showing that whites who currently live in southern states that had high slave populations in the 1860s are more likely to express racial resentment toward blacks.**

- **In a Pew Research survey published in August 2013, men were more likely than women to say that the United States has made significant progress toward equality in the past 150 years (50 percent versus 41 percent).**

- **A Rasmussen Reports survey published in July 2013 found that 30 percent of Americans view race relations as good or excellent.**

Source Notes

Introduction: Is Racism a Thing of the Past?

1. Martin Luther King Jr., "I Have a Dream," Washington, DC, August 28, 1963, National Archives and Records Administration. www.archives.gov.
2. Anti-Defamation League, "What Is Racism?," 2001. http://archive.adl.org.
3. Bobby Jindal, "The End of Race," *Politico,* August 25, 2013. www.politico.com.
4. Jessica Wong, "Racism in America Hasn't Disappeared," *Herald Sun*, October 29, 2013. www.heraldsun.com.
5. Quoted in *USA Today*, "AP Poll: U.S. Majority Have Prejudice Against Blacks," October 27, 2012. www.usatoday.com.
6. Pew Research Center, "King's Dream Remains an Elusive Goal; Many Americans See Racial Disparities," Pew Research Social & Demographic Trends, August 22, 2013. www.pewsocialtrends.org.
7. Pew Research Center, "King's Dream Remains an Elusive Goal."
8. Quoted in *USA Today*, "AP Poll."

Chapter One: What Are the Origins of the Racism Conflict?

9. Quoted in National Humanities Center, "Becoming American: The British Atlantic Colonies, 1690–1763," 2009. http://nationalhumanitiescenter.org.
10. Do Something, "Background on Racial Discrimination," 2012. www.dosomething.org.
11. US Department of State Office of the Historian, "Milestones: 1830–1860." https://history.state.gov.
12. John Burnett, "John Burnett's Story of the Trail of Tears," Cherokee Nation, December 11, 1890. www.cherokee.org.
13. Burnett, "John Burnett's Story of the Trail of Tears."
14. PBS, "The Terrible Transformation." www.pbs.org.
15. Howard Zinn, "1619–1741: Slavery and Slave Rebellion in the US," Libcom.org, February 21, 2011. http://libcom.org.
16. David Brion Davis, *Inhuman Bondage: The Rise and Fall of Slavery in the New World.* New York: Oxford University Press, 2006, p. 1.
17. History.com, "Slavery in America," 2009. www.history.com.

18. History.com, "Slavery in America."
19. Library of Congress, "Immigration: Japanese." www.loc.gov.
20. Paul Spickard, *Japanese Americans: The Formation and Transformations of an Ethnic Group*. Piscataway, NJ: Rutgers University Press, 2009, p. 102.
21. Quoted in Spickard, *Japanese Americans*, p. 107.
22. Quoted in Michelle Miller, "George Takei on a Rueful Journey Back in Time," CBS News, August 4, 2013. www.cbsnews.com.
23. Quoted in Miller, "George Takei on a Rueful Journey Back in Time."
24. Henry Kittredge Norton, *The Story of California from the Earliest Days to the Present*. Chicago, IL: AC McClurg, 1924, pp. 283–96.

Chapter Two: How Common Is Racial Profiling in Law Enforcement?

25. Keith Rushing, "Dissecting the Long, Deep Roots of Racial Profiling in America," *HuffPost Black Voices* (blog), March 1, 2013. www.huffingtonpost.com.
26. Rushing, "Dissecting the Long, Deep Roots of Racial Profiling in America."
27. Daniel Bergner, "Is Stop-and-Frisk Worth It?," *Atlantic*, March 2014. www.theatlantic.com.
28. Quoted in Chris Francescani, Janet Roberts, and Melanie Hicken, "'Stop and Frisk' Polarizes New York," Reuters, July 3, 2012. www.huffingtonpost.com.
29. Michael Bloomberg, "'Stop and Frisk' Is Not Racial Profiling," *Washington Post*, August 18, 2013. www.washingtonpost.com.
30. Quoted in Sara Maria Glanowski, "Growing Up with Stop-and-Frisk," *Atlantic*, August 2013. www.theatlantic.com.
31. Bloomberg, "'Stop and Frisk' Is Not Racial Profiling."
32. Shira A. Scheindlin, "United States District Court, Southern District of New York, David Floyd et al. Against the City of New York," August 12, 2013. www.nysd.uscourts.gov.
33. Quoted in Matt Sledge, "David Floyd, Lead Stop and Frisk Plaintiff, Takes Stand in First Day of Trial," *Huffington Post*, March 18, 2013. www.huffingtonpost.com.
34. Quoted in Sledge, "David Floyd, Lead Stop and Frisk Plaintiff, Takes Stand in First Day of Trial."
35. Scheindlin, "United States District Court, Southern District of New York, David Floyd et al. Against the City of New York."
36. Charlie Brown and Amanda Jantzi, "Driving While Black," Cornell University Law School, 2010. http://courses2.cit.cornell.edu.
37. Quoted in Aaron Mueller, "Traffic Stops by Kalamazoo Police Down by Nearly Half in 6 Months Since Racial Profiling Study," *Kalamazoo Gazette*, March 3, 2014. www.mlive.com.

38. Rushing, "Dissecting the Long, Deep Roots of Racial Profiling in America."
39. Shoshana Hebshi, "'Racially Profiled and Cuffed in Detroit'—Personal Account of Woman Removed from Airplane That Originated in San Diego this Past Sept. 11th," OB Rag, September 13, 2011. http://obrag.org.
40. Quoted in Niraj Warikoo, "Ohio Woman Sues FBI, Airline for Racial Profiling," *USA Today*, January 22, 2013. www.usatoday.com.
41. Quoted in Khalil AlHajal, "Lawyer for Woman Strip-Searched at Detroit Metro Airport: 'She Didn't Have to Go Through This Degrading Experience,'" *Detroit Free Press*, January 23, 2013. www.mlive.com.
42. Quoted in Glanowski, "Growing Up with Stop-and-Frisk."

Chapter Three: How Serious a Problem Is Housing Discrimination?

43. Quoted in Braden Goyette, "The Most Racist Part of Donald Sterling's Legacy Can't Be Solved with a Lifetime Ban," *Huffington Post*, April 30, 2014. www.huffingtonpost.com.
44. Leadership Conference on Civil and Human Rights, "How We Got Here: The Historical Roots of Housing Segregation," December 2008. www.civilrights.org.
45. Quoted in Dmitri Mehlhorn, "A Requiem for Blockbusting: Law, Economics, and Race-Based Real Estate Speculation," *Fordham Law Review*, 1998. http://ir.lawnet.fordham.edu.
46. Leadership Conference on Civil and Human Rights, "How We Got Here."
47. Arnold R. Hirsch, "Blockbusting," *Encyclopedia of Chicago*, 2005. www.encyclopedia.chicagohistory.org.
48. Hirsch, "Blockbusting."
49. History.com, "Fair Housing Act of 1968." www.history.com.
50. History.com, "Fair Housing Act of 1968."
51. Quoted in George Gonzalez, "Racial and Ethnic Minorities Face More Subtle Housing Discrimination," HUD news release, June 11, 2013. http://portal.hud.gov.
52. Quoted in Suzanne Gamboa, "Housing Discrimination Persists Subtly for Minorities, HUD Study Finds," *Huffington Post*, June 11, 2013. www.huffingtonpost.com.
53. Quoted in Ronda Kaysen, "Racial Discrimination in Renting?," *New York Times*, February 14, 2014. www.nytimes.com.
54. National Fair Housing Alliance, *Fair Housing in a Changing Nation*, April 30, 2012. www.nationalfairhousing.org.
55. National Fair Housing Alliance, "Investigation Reveals Discrimination Against Latino Borrowers by Bank of America in Charleston," February 18, 2014. www.nationalfairhousing.org.

56. Denver Metro Fair Housing Center, *Access Denied: A Report on Rental Housing Discrimination in the Denver Metro Area*, February 2014. http://dmfhc.org.
57. Denver Metro Fair Housing Center, *Access Denied.*
58. Quoted in Kristen Leigh Painter, "Study: Discrimination Prevalent in Metro Housing Market," *Denver Post*, February 6, 2014. www.denverpost.com.

Chapter Four: Are Affirmative Action Programs Justified?

59. Lyndon B. Johnson, "Equal Opportunity Is Not Enough," commencement address at Howard University, June 4, 1965. www.pbs.org.
60. Quoted in Office of Equal Opportunity and Diversity, "A Brief History of Affirmative Action," May 3, 2010. www.ocod.uci.edu.
61. David W. DeBruin et al., "Brief for Amici Curiae," 2012. www.americanbar.org.
62. DeBruin et al., "Brief for Amici Curiae."
63. Ben Carson, "Beyond Affirmative Action to Colorblindness," *Washington Times*, February 18, 2014. www.washingtontimes.com.
64. Carson, "Beyond Affirmative Action to Colorblindness."
65. Berneta Hayes, "Affirmative Action Helped Me and Benefits Society (Essay)," Inside Higher Ed, March 12, 2013. www.insidehighered.com.
66. Hayes, "Affirmative Action Helped Me and Benefits Society (Essay)."
67. Lewis F. Powell, "*Regents of the University of California v. Bakke*," June 28, 1978. www.law.cornell.edu.
68. Quoted in Todd J. Gillman, "Abigail Fisher Claims Victory in UT Affirmative Action Case," *Dallas News Trailblazer* (blog), June 24, 2013. http://trailblazersblog.dallasnews.com.
69. Jeffrey M. Jones, "In U.S., Most Reject Considering Race in College Admissions," Gallup, July 24, 2013. www.gallup.com.
70. Richard Sander and Stuart Taylor Jr., "The Painful Truth About Affirmative Action," *Atlantic*, October 2, 2012. www.theatlantic.com.
71. Sander and Taylor, "The Painful Truth About Affirmative Action."
72. Sander and Taylor, "The Painful Truth About Affirmative Action."
73. Quoted in Dan Slater, "Does Affirmative Action Do What It Should?," *New York Times*, March 16, 2013. www.nytimes.com.

Chapter Five: What Progress Has Been Made in the Fight Against Racism?

74. Terrance Heath, "The GOP Can't Get Off the Hook by Declaring the 'End' of Racism," Campaign for America's Future, December 9, 2013. http://ourfuture.org.

75. Eadie Harley, interview with author, March 1, 2014.
76. Harley, interview.
77. Quoted in Scholastic Teacher, "Interview with Rosa Parks," January/ February 1997. http://teacher.scholastic.com.
78. Scholastic Teacher, "Interview with Rosa Parks."
79. Quoted in Henry Ford Museum, "The Story Behind the Bus," 2002. www.thehenryford.org.
80. Quoted in History.com, "Civil Rights Act." www.history.com.
81. History.com, "Civil Rights Act."
82. History.com, "Civil Rights Act."
83. John Hawkins, "15 Moronic Things Liberals Call Racism Since Obama Was Elected," Town Hall, August 27, 2013. http://townhall .com.
84. Heath, "The GOP Can't Get Off the Hook by Declaring the 'End' of Racism."
85. Baratunde Thurston, "Ways White People of Goodwill (and Anyone Else) Can Help End Racism," *Baratunde Blog*, September 21, 2013. http://baratunde.com.
86. Quoted in Scott Jaschik, "Student's Video Leads to Discussion of Race at UCLA," Inside Higher Ed, November 22, 2013. www .insidehighered.com.
87. Quoted in Rahim Kanani, "How Do We Eliminate Racism and Empower Women Around the World?," *Forbes*, July 1, 2013. www .forbes.com.
88. Quoted in Kanani, "How Do We Eliminate Racism and Empower Women Around the World?"
89. Quoted in Charles Hallman, "Courageous Conversations Program, Used in Some Twin Cities Schools to Lower Suspension Rate, Confronts Systemic Racism in Education," *Twin Cities Daily Planet*, July 11, 2013. www.tcdailyplanet.net.
90. Quoted in Hallman, "Courageous Conversations Program, Used in Some Twin Cities Schools to Lower Suspension Rate, Confronts Systemic Racism in Education."

Related Organizations and Websites

American-Arab Anti-Discrimination Committee
1990 M St. NW, Suite 610
Washington, DC 20036
phone: (202) 244-2990
fax: (202) 333-3980
e-mail: adc@adc.org
website: www.adc.org

The American-Arab Anti-Discrimination Committee is a civil rights organization committed to defending the rights of people of Arab descent and promoting their cultural heritage. Its website offers press releases, news articles, and a search engine that produces numerous publications about discrimination and racism.

American Association for Affirmative Action
888 Sixteenth St. NW, Suite 800
Washington, DC 20006
phone: (202) 349-9855
website: www.affirmativeaction.org

The American Association for Affirmative Action is a national association of professionals who work in the areas of affirmative action, equal opportunity, and diversity. Its website offers information about the history of affirmative action, news releases, and a link to the group's blog, where numerous articles about affirmative action are published.

American Civil Liberties Union (ACLU)

125 Broad St., 18th Floor
New York, NY 10004
phone: (212) 549-2500
e-mail: infoaclu@aclu.org
website: www.aclu.org

The ACLU works with courts, legislatures, and communities to defend and preserve the rights and liberties that are guaranteed for all Americans under the US Constitution. Its website offers a wealth of information on racism-related topics, including racial profiling, race and criminal justice, and discrimination, among others.

Anti-Defamation League

823 United Nations Plaza
New York, NY 10017
phone: (212) 885-7700
website: www.adl.org

The Anti-Defamation League fights anti-Semitism and all forms of bigotry, defends democratic ideals, and protects civil rights for all. Its website offers news articles, information sheets on a variety of topics, podcasts, and a search engine that produces numerous articles about racism, discrimination, and other related topics.

Anti-Racist Alliance

351 W. Fifty-Third St.
New York, NY 10019
phone: (212) 957-5305
website: www.antiracistalliance.com

The Anti-Racist Alliance is a grassroots organization that works to achieve racial equality. Its website offers a collection of materials on racism-related topics as well as a bibliography and links to the group's blog and Facebook page.

Center for the Healing of Racism

3821 Caroline St., Suite 102
PO Box 27327
Houston, TX 77227-7327
phone: (713) 520-8226
e-mail: info@centerhealingracism.org
website: www.centerhealingracism.org

The Center for the Healing of Racism seeks to end racism through education in order to empower people and bring positive change to communities. Its website offers a collection of articles on racism-related topics as well as videos, a history page that describes the group's accomplishments, and a photo gallery.

Equal Justice Initiative

122 Commerce St.
Montgomery, AL 36104
phone: (334) 269-1803
fax: (334) 269-1806
e-mail: contact_us@eji.org
website: www.eji.org

The Equal Justice Initiative provides legal representation to indigent defendants and prisoners who have not been treated fairly by the legal system. Its website offers a large collection of news articles, fact sheets, reports, and videos related to racism and the justice system.

Everyday Democracy

111 Founders Plaza, Suite 1403
East Hartford, CT 06108
phone: (860) 928-2616
fax: (860) 928-3713
e-mail: info@everyday-democracy.org
website: www.everyday-democracy.org

Everyday Democracy helps people talk and work together to resolve issues such as racial equity, poverty reduction, economic development, education reform, and building strong neighborhoods. Its website offers a wide variety of publications that support the achievement of these goals.

National Association for the Advancement of Colored People (NAACP)

4805 Mt. Hope Dr.
Baltimore, MD 21215
phone: (410) 580-5777
toll-free: (877) 622-2798
e-mail: info@naacp.org
website: www.naacp.org

The NAACP is the oldest and largest civil rights organization in the United States. Its website offers a large collection of publications and reports, an interactive timeline of NAACP history and notable milestones in the fight against racism, and a link to the organization's blog.

People's Institute for Survival and Beyond

601 N. Carrollton
New Orleans, LA 70119
phone: (504) 301-9292
fax: (504) 301-9291
email: tiphanie@pisab.org
website: www.pisab.org

The People's Institute for Survival and Beyond is a multiracial, antiracist network dedicated to ending racism and other forms of institutional oppression. Its website offers the principles of undoing racism, testimonials, and information on news and events.

Southern Poverty Law Center

400 Washington Ave.
Montgomery, AL 36104
phone: (334) 956-8200
e-mail: info@splcenter.org
website: www.splcenter.org

The Southern Poverty Law Center is dedicated to fighting hate and bigotry and to seeking justice for the most vulnerable people in society. Its website's search engine produces numerous articles, reports, and other publications about racism and related topics.

Vera Institute of Justice

233 Broadway, 12th Floor
New York, NY 10279
phone: (212) 334-1300
fax: (212) 941-9407
e-mail: info@vera.org
website: www.vera.org

The Vera Institute of Justice is an independent, nonpartisan organization dedicated to justice policy and practice. Its website offers numerous racism-related materials, including reports, articles, news releases, and a link to the *Current Thinking* blog.

Additional Reading

Books

Francisco Bethencourt, *Racisms: From the Crusades to the Twentieth Century*. Princeton, NJ: Princeton University Press, 2013.

Eduardo Bonilla-Silva, *Racism Without Racists: Color-Blind Racism and the Persistence of Racial Inequality in America*. Lanham, MD: Rowman and Littlefield, 2014.

Tanner Colby, *Some of My Best Friends Are Black*. New York: Penguin, 2012.

David Brion Davis, *The Problem of Slavery in the Age of Emancipation*. New York: Knopf, 2014.

Joe R. Feagin and José A. Cobas, *Latinos Facing Racism: Discrimination, Resistance, and Endurance*. Boulder, CO: Paradigm, 2013.

Abraham H. Foxman and Christopher Wolf, *Viral Hate*. New York: Palgrave Macmillan, 2013.

Daria Roithmayr, *Reproducing Racism*. New York: New York University Press, 2014.

Richard H. Sander and Stuart Taylor Jr., *Mismatch: How Affirmative Action Hurts Students It's Intended to Help, and Why Universities Won't Admit It*. New York: Basic Books, 2012.

Periodicals

Devon W. Carbado, Cheryl I. Harris, and Kimberle Williams Crenshaw, "Racial Profiling Lives On," *New York Times*, August 14, 2013.

Rahim Kanani, "How Do We Eliminate Racism and Empower Women Around the World?," *Forbes*, July 1, 2013.

Brent Schrotenboer, "Black NFL Players Arrested Nearly 10 Times as Often as Whites," *USA Today*, November 29, 2013.

Gary Shelton, "Sadly, Racism in Sports Won't Go Away," *Tampa Bay (FL) Times*, August 12, 2013.

A.J. Vicens and Brett Brownell, "Share These Stats About Black America with the Racist in Your Life," *Mother Jones*, February 19, 2014.

Richard Winton, "Judge Alleges Racial Profiling by UCLA Police in $10-Million Claim," *Los Angeles Times*, February 3, 2014.

Internet Sources

Jennifer Fratello, Andrés F. Rengifo, and Jennifer Trone, "Coming of Age with Stop and Frisk: Experiences, Self-Perceptions, and Public Safety Implications," Vera Institute of Justice, September 19, 2013. www.vera.org/pubs/special/stop-and-frisk-reports.

George Gonzalez, "Racial and Ethnic Minorities Face More Subtle Housing Discrimination," US Department of Housing and Urban Development, June 11, 2013. http://portal.hud.gov/hudportal/HUD?src=/press/press_releases_media_advisories/2013/HUDNo.13-091.

Nikole Hannah-Jones, "Living Apart: How the Government Betrayed a Landmark Civil Rights Law," ProPublica, November 2, 2013. www.propublica.org/series/living-apart.

Ted Hesson, "Do Pot Arrests in D.C. Equal Racial Profiling?," Fusion, March 5, 2014. http://fusion.net/justice/story/pot-arrests-dc-equal-racial-profiling-417827.

Jareen Imam, "50 Years After King, Hidden Racism Lives On," CNN, August 26, 2013. www.cnn.com/interactive/2013/08/us/everyday-racism.

David Dante Troutt, "The Racism That Still Plagues America," *Salon*, January 20, 2014. www.salon.com/2014/01/20/the_racism_that_still_plagues_america.

Index

Note: Boldface page numbers indicate illustrations.

Picture Credits

AP Images: 11, 60, 68

© Richard Baker/In Pictures/Corbis: 51

© Bettmann/Corbis: 42

© Corbis: 21

© Kevin Downs/Corbis: 28

© Mannie Garcia/Reuters/Corbis: 72

© Richard Levine/Demotix/Corbis: 76

© Pete Marovich/Corbis: 63

Picture History/Newscom: 16

© David Sailors/Corbis: 56

© SuperStock/Corbis: 46

© Seth Wenig/AP/Corbis: 33

About the Author

Peggy J. Parks holds a bachelor of science degree from Aquinas College in Grand Rapids, Michigan, where she graduated magna cum laude. An author who has written more than a hundred educational books for children and young adults, Parks lives in Muskegon, Michigan, a town that she says inspires her writing because of its location on the shores of Lake Michigan.